The Doctor & I

A celebration of a fandom 50 years in the making...

compiled by

WhovianNet.co.uk

The Doctor & I

published in Great Britain by

GJB PUBLISHING

18 Yeend Close
West Molesey,
Surrey KT8 2NY

www.GJBpublishing.co.uk
@GJBpublishing

ISBN 978-0-9576242-4-5

© WhovianNet
www.WhovianNet.co.uk
@WhovianNet

Contents

Foreword

By Richard Curtis

I wasn't a huge fan of Doctor Who when I was young. I'd happily watch it, of course, but my main memories are of my little brother getting terrified, and then of him going to a party dressed as Jon Pertwee in the most ridiculous purple silk shirt and blonde wig. I'm not sure anyone ever spoke to him at school again. But, as a writer, lots of things about Doctor Who are inspiring.

First, it's that wonderful link with our past. It's like being able to write an actual *Beatles* or *Take That* song. Then for some writers, like me, it's the one chance to work on something that's science fiction. And then it's the extraordinary range of things you can do with that - from sheer excitement to proper fear to striving for meaning and, ultimately, trying to say something about being human.

My own Doctor Who episode, *Vincent and the Doctor*, began its life when I had an idea whilst writing a TV film called *Bernard and the Genie*. It was about someone travelling back in time to tell Van Gogh how great he would become. I didn't use it, but I remembered it. Then Steven Moffat approached me and I took the offer extremely seriously because my children and I were at that time huge fans of the new generation of Doctor Who. And so I worked out how I might be able to use the Van Gogh story, not only as something exciting, but also as a way to talk about depression and mental illness, something that still isn't discussed or understood too much.

My one piece of big advice for aspiring writers is try to write about something that really matters to you. In this case, it was my interest in mental illness and my real passion for the work of, and interest in, the life of Van Gogh. Whenever in life I've written about things that I think might just amuse or interest other people, but that aren't quite my bag, it has always been a disaster. But, thankfully, I know quite a lot about the subject of depression and so there were all sorts of things I hoped I could portray and hint at. I think in this case, however, the real praise has to go to Tony Curran, who acted the part. He is a completely brilliant actor - serious, proper - and I think he managed to take all the simple things I had written and give them that real depth, meaning and emotion.

Whilst writing the episode, I felt comforted knowing that it was one of the Doctor Who sub-genres - the meeting with historical figures. That's one of the great charms of the job - you're free, but at the same time you're working to a brief. There are lots of things you can make up but at the same time there are lots of things that you can't change. I often think of the phrase *'service is perfect freedom'* and I thought of it a lot when I was writing Doctor Who.

As it enters its 50th year, the factors behind its ongoing success are as endless as the Universe itself. Randomly, here are three things.

Firstly, the casting has always been completely wonderful, particularly in the new era. Serious, not condescending, quirky, brave, interesting. This applies to both the leads and the supporting characters - there's always a real integrity and imagination there.

Secondly, I like the transmission time in the UK. Early Saturday evening, when the whole family is together. It's brought us together and given us so many happy and scary and interesting and exciting and wondrous times over the years.

Thirdly, it's the fearlessness. That willingness to use the fact that it's a long running series, to not find a formula and stick to it, but to still go out on a limb, to do different things, to play things out at different lengths. After all, who would imagine that one of the greatest ever episodes, *Blink*, should hardly feature the Doctor in it at all...?

Introduction

For the last 50 years, Doctor Who has captivated generations of fans all over the world. Saturday 23rd November 2013 will not only mark five decades of this now internationally acclaimed series, but also half a century of its accompanying fandom, the oldest members of which have been by the Doctor's side since the TARDIS first opened its doors on that cold winter night back in 1963...

Doctor Who fans - affectionately referred to as the 'Whovians' - are universally renowned for their enthusiasm and dedication. WhovianNet's own definition of the term 'Whovian', located on our 'About' page, describes one as 'an overly obsessed fan of the Doctor Who franchise', because if there's one trait you need on your resumé to become an honourary Whovian, it is just that. You need to be obsessed. Well and truly, actually.

To elaborate, Whovians don't just watch Doctor Who. Oh no, that would be daft. Whovians live, breathe and dream it. A typical 'day in the life of a Whovian' consists of re-watching episodes, scouring the Internet for the latest news (hopefully on WhovianNet - *ahem*!) and generally spending countless hours discussing and dissecting the lives and times of everybody's favourite Time Lord amongst a growing mass collection of figures, memorabilia and that TARDIS mug your friend/colleague got you for a Secret Santa last year that you casually laughed at but secretly it's the best thing you've ever owned.

But just what is it about the Doctor Who phenomena that continues to enthral fans young and old after all these years? With its ever changing genres, themes and characters, even its lead actor can get replaced when the time comes to give the show its latest reboot. Perhaps that in itself is the reason behind Doctor Who's longevity - that constantly old yet constantly new format that means it's never in danger of becoming stale or predictable. Every so often the show gets flipped upside down but at its heart (or should that be 'hearts'?) remains that lonely old Time Lord, the ultimate hero, the man who keeps running because he's got nowhere to run to. Actress Louise Jameson, who portrayed the Fourth Doctor's leather clad barbarian warrior companion Leela in the 70's, once told us in an interview that the Doctor has "single-handedly made being a geek trendy". We couldn't agree more, and, from the bottom of our Whovian hearts, we can't thank him enough.

Running a Doctor Who fansite means that over the years we have experienced first hand just how much Doctor Who means to its fans. Our inbox, news blog and Twitter feed are regularly inundated with opinions, comments and reactions from people all over the world who continue to be impacted and inspired by the show. Everyone has something to say about Doctor Who and, as we write this (coincidentally, and rather appropriately, on our sixth birthday, 9th October 2013), we are both proud and humbled - 'pumbled' - that so many of you have chosen WhovianNet as your place to say it. Thanks for sticking with us!

We're sure if the secret behind Doctor Who's success was known we'd all be bottling it up and making our own shows about gas masked zombie children, dinosaurs on spaceships and mutated metal monsters bent on world domination. Until its secret is discovered, however, we'll simply leave it at this. Doctor Who makes people happy. Whether you stay up until 4am because "just one episode" turns into eight more (we've all been there, right?) or you spend your spare time attending conventions dressed up as your favourite character or monster (again, we've all been there!), it's that sense of being part of such a far-reaching community that generally makes the Whovian fandom such a brilliant place to be. And now, as we mark its tremendous 50th anniversary (time flies when you're having fun!), we're honoured to be able to bring you our own collection of your Whovian memoirs, a unique insight into our weird and wonderful Doctor Who fandom as told over 86 heartfelt and heartwarming stories detailing, in an nutshell, what Who means to... well, you.

Before we get started, we'd just like to say a huge thank you to everyone who has helped us with the creation of this book. We were completely overwhelmed by the response it had and whether you helped spread the word or contributed to the project directly or both, we really couldn't have done any of it without all of your help and enthusiasm. We're extremely proud of what we've put together and we hope this book you're holding in your hands serves as a heartfelt reminder of just what makes our Whovian family so fantastic. Because that's what it's all about, right?

After all, we've all got a 'The Doctor & I' story. It's time to read yours.

50 Years Later...

By Jane Hains, aged 61, from England

When I was eleven years old, back in 1963, I was introduced to an extraordinary character known simply as 'the Doctor'. In those days there was usually a family serial on television around Saturday tea time. My Dad had always enjoyed science fiction and had read all about Doctor Who in the Radio Times. He gathered me, my Mum and my younger brother in the front room in front of our black and white television ready for it to begin. I wasn't sure what to expect really. I remember hearing that theme music for the first time and there was just something so different about it. And then there was the Doctor, an old man who seemed so strict with a very modern granddaughter called Susan (such an ordinary name for a traveller from a different world...), who lived in a police box. But oh, what a police box - it was *bigger on the inside*! With that my imagination was grabbed and I couldn't wait to see what Susan's teachers would think when they followed her home. Then, the adventure started and Doctor Who immediately became a programme my family just had to watch.

And then came the Daleks. Of all those early creatures, it is the Daleks I liked best. They weren't just men dressed in strange suits or bubble wrap - they were so different from anything I had ever seen before. Even as an adult, and when I visited the Doctor Who Exhibition in Blackpool and saw a Dalek close up for the first time, they still make me feel uncomfortable, like I can't really trust what I know to be true... 'Exterminate!'

Over the years Doctor Who has continued to find new ways of surprising me, especially when the Doctor regenerated for the first time. The Second Doctor was funny and mischievous and because of this he quickly became my favourite. There was new companions, too and I could easily relate to Jamie's wonder at seeing all those futuristic contraptions.

Even when I eventually moved to college I remained devoted to the series. Every Saturday night I'd be in the students' union TV lounge and a career in residential child care followed which meant I'd frequently enjoy Doctor Who with the younger children. By this point it had, sadly, stopped appealing to my imagination, but I will always be a faithful viewer with a soft spot for William Hartnell...

In 2005 the series returned and there I was once again, just like I had been all those years ago, sitting, in my own front room this time, waiting for it to come on. I was full of hopeful expectations while also thinking that it could never be as good as it had been. How wrong I was! The moment arrived and there was that signature tune, modernised but unmistakably Doctor Who. From that moment I was almost certain it was going to be alright. And it was more. It was more than alright, it was like being that 11 year old child again, having my imagination stretched and delighted. With the modern Doctors, Doctor Who has become a story with thrills, scares, laughs and tears. Nothing on television has made me cry as much, or as often, as the Tenth Doctor's final scenes.

I don't suppose I will be around to celebrate its 100th birthday but I shall be watching for as long as I can - intrigued, delighted, saddened and amazed, all of the emotions that link me to my childhood years long ago.

So here's to my future, and my past, shared with the Doctor.

Adventures In An Old Blue Box

By Steven Roy Evans, aged 60 and a bit, from Cambridge, UK

What does Doctor Who mean to me? Well, quite a lot actually. I was ten years old when *An Unearthly Child* broke the bonds of what constituted children's television. In a decade when the human race was taking its first tottering steps beyond our planet, when Swinging Britain led the world in cool fashion and music, and when the foundations of what we now recognise as a multi-cultural society were being laid, the genius of a handful of forward-thinking BBC producers opened the door to an infinity of adventure, times and places that not even the big screens of Hollywood had contemplated exploring.

From his first foray onto our screens, the Doctor, with his companions, plunged us directly into the realities and struggles of life. The joys, the heartaches, the noble acts and the ultimate sacrifices. I watched that first episode alone, a thick November fog swirling outside the window to match the ones through which Susan Foreman liked to walk. Even the grainy 405 lines of our TV couldn't diminish the excitement of following Barbara through the TARDIS' doors into the Doctor's awesome world...

It hooked me completely. This was something new, something so completely different. It shone in the heavens like a radiant star. There was no boring old rocket ship for our hero - his vessel could go anywhere and everywhere which meant the canvas on which his adventures appeared was as infinitely huge as his time machine. Each opening of the TARDIS' doors heralded another marvellous four or six episodes of wonder, followed by the frustration of a cliffhanger ending which provided a week of speculation in the school playground (and acted-out possible scenarios which were never, ever correct!).

My Doctor will always be the First Doctor. He had this abundance. *My* Doctor was the Mystery Man of Time, the lonely exile of the fourth dimension - 'the original, you might say'! No Time Lords, no Gallifrey - our hero was as ignorant as the viewers in each new situation, his learning curve as steep as ours. Infallible? Never. Frustrated? Often. Like my own grandfather, Susan's was grumpy, bossy, intolerant and scathing, and very much loved when you broke through the crusty exterior. This Doctor I understood, the key element in my enjoyment of the programme. For me, the first will always be the very best.

Through the years leading up to the 50th anniversary I have watched, listened to or read all the classic stories. In the mid-1970s, Jon Pertwee had sadly hung up his cloak for the (almost) last time when the Doctor Who Appreciation Society - the only official fan club at that time - came to my attention. I signed up with my friend John Peel (author of several Doctor Who novelisations and original books) and during the summer of 1977 we attended the first historic Doctor Who Convention in the Broomwood Church Hall in Battersea. I had the pleasure of meeting Jon Pertwee, resplendent in full Doctor Who regalia, during the autograph session, and that afternoon we watched a very ill-at-ease Tom Baker and Louise Jameson take to the stage, both wearing that 'where am I, what am I doing here?' expression a lot of people assume in bewildering circumstances. It was around this time John and I both met our future partners, he moving to America and I to Cambridge, where the demands of marriage, career and mortgages put an end to my fan activity or many years.

Sadly, I have to confess that I was not unhappy about the termination of the show in 1989. Sylvester McCoy was a brilliant Doctor, but he was never really given a chance. Poor and confusing stories and unsympathetic characters and situations all conspired to the show's demise. Had the production team, like several before it, recognised they had run out of steam, maybe these fifty years would have been unbroken by that controversial fifteen-year hiatus. Who knows? And really, since 2005 and the Doctor's triumphal renaissance, who cares? The Doctor is back, the TARDIS flies again and we've had eight years of Saturday night entertainment for a whole new generation who have discovered their own sense of wonder for the modern exploits of our mutual hero.

Through the good times and the bad, I have enjoyed Doctor Who. I still rank it as the world's number one adventure show in whatever form it manifests itself, be it TV, radio books, and I cannot actually conceive of anything ever equalling, let alone supplanting, its sheer scope of imagination and originality. As the Eleventh Doctor stands poised to bid us adieu, I look forward to meeting the 12th in this long line of illustrious Lords of Time. The First Doctor launched us into a bold concept of renewal and change when he told Ben and Polly, 'This old body of mine is wearing a bit thin'. Now we wait for the parting epitaph of the outgoing owner of the universe's last surviving TARDIS - a 'Geronimo!' moment if ever there was one.

'Fantastic!'

A Mild Curiosity in a Junkyard

By Nathan Bennett, aged 25, from Australia

At first, there is nothing. Then, a dim shaft of light rises, tearing an opening in the void. An otherworldly tune echoes out as the light opens further. Cascading, drifting, and, finally, resolving into two words...

DOCTOR WHO.

The words are lost in a formless white mist which blends seamlessly into a crisp London fog. Through this fog we see an ordinary junkyard where a wooden box begins to hum.

Yet despite all appearances, this is not November 1963. We're not in the United Kingdom. It's almost forty years later, on the opposite side of the world. But in this impossible time and place, these moments once more become a beginning. My beginning.

Having been born between *Dragonfire* and *Remembrance of the Daleks*, Doctor Who was never a part of my childhood. Any encounter I had with it was only as it echoed in our popular culture, and like all echoes it came through dim and distorted. It wasn't until September 2003 that things began to change. Australia's national broadcaster, the ABC, ran an ad to announce that they would soon be airing episodes of Doctor Who from its very beginning. I was curious. Even though I was in my mid-teens I had never watched a black and white television programme. I was interested in seeing what one would be like. Knowing how badly science-fiction dates, I thought I could get a few chuckles out of some wobbly sets and wobblier monsters and then move on...

I haven't moved on.

How could I? That first cliffhanger! The battered police box from a junkyard standing in a strange new place while an unknown shadow creeps across the alien sand. From its ethereal opening to the introduction of the enigmatic Doctor and his wondrous box to that final image, this was an episode designed to grip its audience and bring them along to an unknown world. And though I may have been forty years too late, I was able to come along as well.

From there, the places they took us only became stranger. A petrified forest on a dead planet. A city of mutated misfits, shrieking in their iron lungs. A swamp filled with tentacled creatures and a treacherous polystyrene cavern. Then, just as we think we know what to expect, we find that the Doctor's ship can be the strangest place of all.

I was enraptured by the adventures of the TARDIS crew, but I had yet to consider myself a fan of the show. Fandom is itself a strange place and requires something special to enter, something that leaves you with no doubt that this show is going to stay with you. For me, that something special is the third episode of *The Keys of Marinus*. No, really. It was the first episode that I was not able to see and did not bother to tape. It was also what made me discover that missing an episode of Doctor Who was something I never wanted to happen again.

If *The Keys of Marinus* marks the time I entered fandom, then it was during *The Ark* when that door closed behind me. Before then I was content to simply watch the episodes as they came on the screen, not giving them a thought after the end credits faded away. But since the last episode Vicki had somehow transformed into a black-haired girl with crusaders' clothes and a volatile accent, and I needed to find out why. For the first time I searched for Doctor Who on the Internet and drowned in a sea of information as its universe opened up to me. Eight Doctors! Twenty-six seasons of adventures! But most amazing of all - the TARDIS was blue! I had somehow managed to become a Doctor Who fan in the 21st century believing that it was brown...

This rush of discovery was soon tempered by that inevitable disappointment as I discovered that the era of the show I was currently watching was largely unavailable. Lost. Missing. Destroyed. With the ABC not showing any episodes from incomplete serials, and skipping *The War Games* due to a ten second Dalek cameo and a wavering rights situation, the Doctor's second form came and went in the blink of an eye. In a matter of weeks, the show I had grown to love disintegrated before me.

How fortunate that with Doctor Who, every ending is a new beginning.

So I continued to journey with the Doctor. Thanks to the Internet I now knew the lay of the land ahead but the show was still able to surprise me. The sudden appearance of colour-separation overlay. Sporadic, inexplicable shifts back into black and white. New companions. New villains. New Doctors. New worlds.

And then, unexpectedly, a new series, though remarkably this was what I was least enthused about. The ads that heralded its arrival were the complete antithesis of what had initially attracted me to Doctor Who – a glut of fast action, computer-generated spectacle and Britney Spears. When *Rose* premiered halfway through *City of Death*, I was relatively unimpressed and instantly relegated the new series as a secondary concern to 'proper', classic era Who. I was one of the youngest old curmudgeons in fandom.

It's only looking back that I can see how perfect *Rose* was for relaunching the series. I appreciate how sophisticated the show's revival was, but at the time I took it for granted. I never had to spend decades waiting for Doctor Who to return. I never knew the shared suffering of the wilderness years. Doctor Who came to me as an endless stream of adventure, interrupted only by the Daleks and their lawyers. It was always there - 5:30 p.m., Monday to Thursday, week in and week out.

Try as I might, I cannot find the words to encompass everything I get from Doctor Who. Doctor Who is not just one story. It's a universe of stories. Not just stories of alien worlds and alien times, but also the story of how television, how our culture, has developed over the past five decades. It's the story of the people whose work built the show, and it's the story of the people who adore it. And no matter where or when I find myself, there's always one of these stories that I want to hear. It supplements every day of my life with adventure, humour and mad invention. It's something that will always interest, amuse and inspire me.

And it all started out as a mild curiosity.

The Most Cunning Trap in Time and Space

By Tyler English, aged 18, from the USA

How my Doctor Who adventure started is an interesting tale. Looking back, I realise how woven into my life this show really is. Most people my age would generally hear about the revived series and be brought in watching that, and for some, that's the only Doctor Who they care to watch. Me? I had the rare exception of starting off with the very first Doctor, in the Target novelization of *The Dalek Invasion of Earth*. The book had a beautiful cover illustration of what I would later learn was the most feared being in all the cosmos. My great aunt gave me this book several years ago when I was about 9, and it has stuck in the back of my head ever since.

Two years passed, and as I heard rumblings of some new sci-fi show coming to PBS that appeared to be a man in a leather jacket running from a fireball, I still hadn't come in contact with the show. I was in my public library when I stumbled upon a DVD copy of *Robot*. I took it home in ecstatic glee, thinking I'd finally found this allusive TV show.

As an 11 year old kid, what I saw at first glance disappointed me. But as I stuck with it, past the silly robot and the incredibly bright lighting, I saw a charm and whimsy that mesmerized me in the form of a man with a ridiculously long scarf. A few months passed and I returned to the library, to that same shelf. But what I saw looked quite a bit newer, and could possibly scare me to death... I grabbed the Series 1 box set, and less ecstatic than the first time, I was determined to give it another go.

And that was it. There was no way out. The trap laid throughout my history had finally ensnared me. I blazed through Series 1 and 2 and happened to learn about a thing called the Internet along the way. Series 3 had just finished and was arriving at my library. I knew I had to be the first one to get it or I'd be late for the sure to be incredible Series 4.

As time passed, I can finally see the magnitude of this trap. My father watched when he was a kid, my mother had seen it, and even my grandmother had seen it. So why did no one tell *me* about it? I'm convinced history was conspiring against me. Knowing more about the show now I see just how much we're connected. My favourite authors, comic book illustrators and actors all have ties to this show. I even have the same birthday as William Hartnell. I've spent more money than I care to calculate on books,

DVDs, memorabilia, autographs, conventions, and the occasional TARDIS replica. Ah, the TARDIS. Don't even get me started on how beautiful that blue box looks...

I live in an age where the show is almost more popular than ever. Anyone I talk to has at least heard about it. I've done what I can, of course. I've created as much awareness as I can by telling people about it and lending my DVDs. I've gotten my neighbours hooked. But this show has been around for 50 years and will be around for much longer than that. Who knows where it will when the time comes for me to leave this Earth? I'd like to think that I'd have one last good chat about it with a complete stranger before I go. Just me and some bloke, talking about that wildly popular and spectacular show

I'm proud to say I've seen the majority of the Classic series and all of the New series. It's changed so much about me. This wonderful, ridiculous and mad show has shaped me for the better. It's taught me that even the most ordinary person is the most important thing in the universe, even when that universe is ever contracting and expanding and is full of so much wonder. It's taught me to hope, to see the best in people, to think, to use words instead of violence, and to enjoy life. Whether that life is running down corridors from monsters, or being just an ordinary person from Earth, we're all magnificent.

We're all fantastic.

Something Special

By Linzi Osburn, aged 49, from Lancashire, UK

I share something special with the Doctor. Both he and I turn 50 this year.

I remember my introduction to the Doctor as a young child, sitting curled up on the couch with my parents in 1968. Patrick Troughton appeared on the screen and I can honestly say I was hooked. I immediately loved everything about the Doctor and his adventures and even as a 5 year I would wait patiently each week to see what would happen next. Of course, back then the episodes all ran together and it would often take 10 or more episodes before you'd have the ending - having a cliffhanger each week would drive my parents crazy when I'd repeatedly ask, *"When is Doctor Who on?"*!

But I've never missed an episode. Even when I moved to Australia and then got married and moved to the US, I would find ways to catch up. More than once the Doctor has 'come to my rescue' and it's by watching episodes I can 'escape' the drama of my own life and envelope myself in his world. I've been able to forget the horrible things going on around me and become a part of the Doctor's adventures for a short while. As I grew up, and even now as an adult, I'm not ashamed to say I'm always hoping to hear the TARDIS land in my yard...

When my husband died in 2007, it was an especially bad time for me as I had just recently lost my father, too. Little did I know, a few short months later I was also to lose my Mum, so I took solace in the Doctor. By that time I'd already amassed a huge collection of Doctor Who memorabilia, from books to sonic screwdrivers, collectible toys, posters, and even a life size stand up poster of David Tennant - now THAT was something to see in my room!

So here I am waiting somewhat impatiently for the anniversary special. I really wish I could have been in London at the time of filming. I just can't wait to see what the future holds. I've had so many happy years of watching Doctor Who and I might be nearly 50, but I'm planning to get a tattoo of the TARDIS on my arm. As I write this, I'm looking at a poster of the TARDIS on my door and if I look *really* hard, maybe one day I'll see that door open.

Thank you, Doctor. Thank you for the adventures, the laughter, the tears, the fun of getting to know the new you each time and thank you for giving me the chance to live vicariously through your adventures.

If you ever need a new companion, I'm right here.

Timey-Wimey

By Jeanette Stent, aged 46, from the UK

I first met the Doctor when I was five. Back then he was silver-haired, wore a cape and had a yellow car. And I thought he was amazing. I looked forward to seeing him every week, even though I often used to end up watching from between my fingers with my hands over my face or from - yes, you guessed it - behind the sofa! My Mum says she used to threaten to turn it off because I was scared and I'd reply, somewhat worriedly, "No, no, don't — I have to see what happens to the Doctor!"

I remember playing Doctor Who at school, pressing imaginary buttons and swishing imaginary capes and scarves. Being quite a bossy child, I was always the Doctor. And then my Doctor changed, but I didn't mind. After the initial shock, I soon realised he was actually still the same - he hadn't really changed at all!

But then came a time when there was no more Doctor Who on the TV and real life intervened for a while. I was always listening out for the sound of TARDIS engines on the breeze. Fast forward to a Saturday evening in March 2005. I'm at work but I manage to get away for ten minutes to watch a new beginning. I'm not alone - the room is full. I shout with delight at the sonic screwdriver and cheer at "I'm the Doctor!" and oh my God - the TARDIS!

And now, it's the 50th anniversary year and Doctor Who is cool. Who knew? Well, I always did (obviously!). And I love it all. My flat is full of sonic screwdrivers, small plastic figures, DVDs, CDs, books and there may even be a life-size cardboard cut-out or two... The Doctor is always there when I need him, and that most definitely *is* cool (as are bow ties!).

My 12 year old niece calls me "Doctor Who freak" and yes, she has a point. But I'm happy with that - oh yes! The Doctor is in. And I'm a very happy Whovian.

Early Memories

By Tim Sandle, aged 45, from London, UK

I'm not sure when I first began to watch Doctor Who. It would have been in the very early 1970s when I was around five years of age. I used to watch it with my grandparents, just after Saturday tea. These early episodes were during the Jon Pertwee era.

My earliest memory, the one that is permanently lodged into my memory, is of the Sea Devils slowing rising out of the sea - those terrifying alien like creatures emerging from the greyish water, dripping wet, with hideous beak-like faces and carrying some kind of ray-gun...

I also have good memories of Jon Pertwee's Doctor. A little bit dashing, flash clothes, lots of gadgets, willing to fight when he needed to. As a character he seemed a little paternal, sometimes harsh, rather like a 'cool' science teacher at the kind of school I wished I could attend. He was also reassuring and someone I knew, in my childhood fantasy of life in the TARDIS, I could rely upon.

Looking back, some of the gadgets and endless car-plane chases that filled up some episodes now seem a little over-dramatic, sometimes getting in the way of the actual story. At this stage, Doctor Who was trying to be too self-consciously cool and feeling the need to draw on the other dramas of the time, things like *Jason King* or even Roger Moore's *James Bond*. Of course, I didn't know this at the time. As a child these gadgets were terribly exciting.

Whilst Jon Pertwee paved the way for my initiation into Doctor Who, it was Tom Baker that I grew up with, seeing me through from the age of seven through to thirteen. He was 'my Doctor'. Mysterious, alien, erratic and unpredictable. I liked the way he often mocked the villains and monsters that he faced, often armed with a jelly baby. He always seemed to pull something unpredictable out of the bag, or rather from the deep pockets of his overcoat as he swept his long, colourful scarf aside and rummaged for a new high device or ball of string!

Tom Baker's portrayal was a Doctor who acted more on his wits and he drew on technology a little less than Pertwee's. Tom Baker's episodes, as I grew up, also seemed more in-depth, more sci-fi, a little more adult. The ethical dilemmas in *Genesis of the Daleks* was a good case of this. Seeing the Doctor holding two wires and weighing up whether to destroy the future Dalek creatures took the programme to a whole new level for me. I also liked Tom Baker's companions, especially Sarah Jane Smith, who had plenty of spirit.

There was a happy day in 1977 when Tom Baker came to my home town for a signing at a local independent bookshop. I remember purchasing a Target book and queuing up in nervous anticipation. I can't remember speaking to Tom Baker, though I do remember him handing out jelly babies. I still have my treasured signed copy, replete with yellowing pages and a slightly torn cover.

To sum up, my memories of Doctor Who began in the 1970s and they are happy ones, tinged with 1970s Technicolor. Although I've continued to watch Doctor Who and I remain a big fan, nothing can beat the sense of childhood wonder of watching, guessing and expecting as, week by week, the episodes unfolded and new and imaginative monsters were revealed...

I Owe It All To My Mum

By Ben Thatcher, aged 18, from the UK

I was either three or four years old when I first discovered the show. It was 1998. The show had been off the air for nine years and my Mum and I were at a charity sale event, I can't exactly remember what it was for, but her eyes turned to a VHS cover. It was of a Dalek on fire with strange brown creatures with big googley eyes chanting around the flames of the dead Dalek. It was *Death to the Daleks*, a Third Doctor and Sarah Jane Smith story. Mum had grown up with the show, the Daleks being her childhood favourite, with Jon Pertwee and Tom Baker being her companions. I had probably watched the McGann movie with her a year before for this reason. I have been told I had, but I don't remember that sadly.

We arrived home and the first thing I did was watch the video. I was captivated by the strange cover and the multi-coloured diamond logo. This was something good. I had to know what it was about. And I was terrified. I didn't just have a behind the sofa moment, I was so terrified I ran to the other end of the house. Yep. I have my Doctor Who horror story which adults seem to have. I was so scared that I hid the video, pretending we lost it at the event so that that Evil Scene could never ever be played again. I went on with my life, almost forgetting about it and the horror I went through at the hands of this television show...

Then came 2005. I was ten years old. I was the man of the house. I was brave. I found the VHS. I remembered the fear as I saw the cover, but, being ten, I was going to be heroic. I put the video in the machine. I pressed play and the sheer quality of Jon Pertwee and Elisabeth Sladen's performances had me glued..

Then, of course, I discovered the Classic Doctor Who DVDs. Mum agreed to buy one, worried I wouldn't like it. The first was *Remembrance of the Daleks*. I was in love when Ace attacked the Dalek with the baseball bat. I wanted more Doctor Who. I *needed* more. *Resurrection of the Daleks*. *The Dalek Invasion of Earth*. *The Five Doctors*. Every single one had me longing for more and more.

Now, eight years later, I have watched all the surviving episodes and regularly attend signings and conventions. I've even converted a few friends. Jon Pertwee's *Death to the Daleks* made me a Whovian. And I owe it all to my Mum. If she hadn't bought that video, well... I can't imagine what my life would be like without this wonderful show.

The Doctor, My Hero

By Adam Chapman, aged 32, from Nottingham, UK

The Doctor saved my life.Yes, he did. Not a doctor, but the Doctor, that lone wanderer from the planet Gallifrey, that mad man with the box.

It all started on a cold and dreary New Year's Day in the late 80s. My family and I were adjusting back to normality after the excesses of Christmas, the baubles were about to be taken down and, even worse, in a few days I would be returning to primary school.

My school days were not happy ones. Children could sense I was different and with difference comes misunderstanding and fear. That empty and hollow fear of returning to school was slowly creeping up on me and I was about to leave the safe refuge of home to face the lion's den once more.

So, as I awoke at the start of the new year, my eyes still misty and my mind drifting away with thoughts of school and the trials and tribulations that would await me there, I heard a familiar voice bellowing to me from the stairs. *"Morning Ad, time to get up... After breakfast it'll be time to bring your Christmas presents to your room..."*

A sense of delight overtook me. I was looking forward to bringing my treasure trove of Christmas gifts to the bedroom that my brother and I shared. I raced down and almost inhaled my breakfast. Once we had all finished, I dashed to the living room and behind the sofa to collect my new belongings. There, just under the windowsill was our shared gift - our very own beautiful, black and white portable television! My Dad carried it up our room and set it up as we packed our gifts away in their new homes. Then, me and my brother settled on our new beanbags in front of the television as Dad twisted the dial. There was a momentary silence and then a dot of white exploded with a flash and, as if by magic, the television switched on.

Enthralled by our new TV, my brother and I were transfixed as an unearthly theme swept the room. *"Dum de dum, dum de dum, dum de dum, dum de dum..."* I was transfixed as swirls and waves of light filled the screen and a face appeared - a man's face with a warm and reassuring smile. Text formed on the screen which read *'Doctor Who'* followed by *'The Sea Devils'*. I was bewitched for the whole episode and by the time the titles rolled, I wanted more.

And so it became my Sunday lunch tradition, watching this strange and eccentric show about an alien warrior, a warrior who would use his wit and intelligence to fight the monsters and evil that the universe would produce.

Meanwhile, school was hard. The bullying would become physical and I would feel such a sense of loneliness and dejection. But for those fleeting moments on a Sunday lunch, I would feel like I *belonged*, like I was part of something. These adventures through time and space would become my escapism as I learnt that there was nothing wrong with being different. After all, the Doctor himself was different - he had two hearts and he could regenerate, but he was still accepted and, most importantly, loved and adored by his allies. I grew to learn that we are all different and we are all so very special, but most importantly that being different is a gift, not a hindrance.

As the 1980s ended, so did my favourite show as Doctor Who was put on hiatus. I left primary school in the early 90s and moved to secondary school, hoping that my new life would see the end of all the bullying and tormenting. But sadly it wasn't meant to be. The bullies followed me to my new school. They found a new circle of friends and my unhappiness increased. Nearly every week I would end up in my head of year's office with a ripped uniform or cuts and newly formed bruises. Without the show I didn't have my escapism and there was nothing else I could watch on TV that connected to me in the way that Doctor Who did. I couldn't talk to people about my problems because I didn't understand them myself.

My school years ended as the TV Movie aired and I loved seeing the return of my hero. I admired how he faced up to his demons, not just the Master, but also to his understanding of who he was post-regeneration. This started to open up my own mind. I started to discover why I was different, that I was attracted to males and, slowly, I realised that I was gay. This was so hard, not knowing anyone else who was gay, but as the years progressed, my confidence slowly grew and I went to bars and clubs and met new friends. And then came March 2005.

On that sunny Saturday afternoon, the TV - now in colour - in my room once again faded. This time, however, an all too familiar image filled the screen. The moon panning out to Earth, then into Europe and London... Doctor Who had arrived in the 21st Century and once again, just like that little boy nearly a couple of decades before, I was bewitched.

And now, for the last eight years, Doctor Who has become such a major part of my life, and as I grew to understand and accept who I was, so did the Doctor. After the desolation of his people and his home planet, the Doctor represented an element that we all possess - we are all different, all unique, all just as important and we all have such potential. A potential to be a force for good, to have the strength to face off our own nightmares and insecurities. Just as the Doctor has had to face Daleks and Slitheen, Cybermen and Sycorax, my battles have been with my identity and depression.

And now, as we celebrate 50 years of the most successful science fiction show on Earth, I thank you, Doctor Who. Not just for providing that escapism I so desperately searched for all those years ago, but also for making me realise that I am not alone, and that, just like every person who inhabits this spinning sphere in the infinity of space, I have the potential to do good and be good, and by God, I'm going to!

So thank you, Doctor, for saving me.

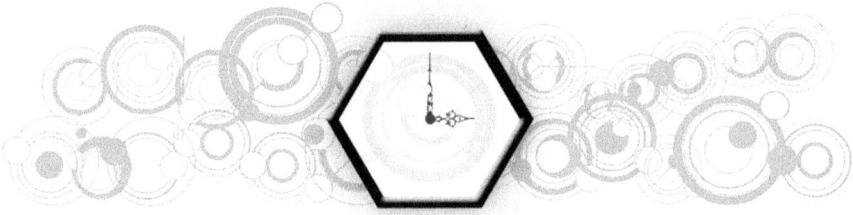

It All Worked Out

By Josh Gardiner, aged 17, from Australia

My parents are English and my Dad used to watch Doctor Who as a child. He always used to make the Doctor Who "knock knock" joke when I was little but I never had any idea what he was talking about. Then one day in 2004, when I was eight years old, I was in the lounge room playing with my toys and I heard this strange sound on the TV. I turned around and saw a man in medieval times walking into a blue box. I was hooked from that moment on, and all my Dad's "knock knock" jokes suddenly made sense. It was on every day at 6:30pm to 7 o'clock and for that half an hour I was glued to the screen. My first Doctor was Jon Pertwee and I'm fairly certain the story I first watched was *The Time Warrior*.

When the new series started in 2005, Doctor Who became a 'family thing'. Every Saturday night we would all watch Doctor Who together. We had a tradition when I was little that Saturday's were 'lolly night' and my brother and I would sit in front of the TV eating the lollies we had chosen and we just wouldn't move.

Up until I was twelve I would dress up in my dressing gown, grab my Sonic Screwdriver and pretend to be David Tennant and play with my figurines. After that I discovered fan fiction and I began to write my own Doctor Who stories, some of which were ideas that I used to act out with my figurines or when I was in my dressing gown. I still collect figurines (and play with them... on occasion...).

I'm seventeen now and I still love Doctor Who as much as the first day I watched it. It taught me that everybody is an individual person and that you shouldn't care what people think because it's okay to be weird. It gave me characters I could identify with and places I wish I could visit. It helped me see that the world is a beautiful, brilliant place. I'm proud to be a nerd in general, but I'm especially proud to be a Whovian.

But the thing that always intrigues me is that I may not have ended up watching it at all. If I didn't turn around a see what was on the TV, I wouldn't have started watching and what if I had turned around and glimpsed a Hartnell or Troughton episode? An old black and white television show wouldn't be that appealing to an eight year old. I turned around at the exact moment on that exact day and saw something that I found interesting. That moment could have gone so many different ways, but it didn't, and I'm glad because, without it, I wouldn't be the person I am today.

Doctor Who has helped me to become me.

A Texan Remembers When (And Who)

By Chris Coker, aged 57, from Paris, Texas, USA

Like many long-time American fans, I first met the Doctor during his fourth incarnation (insert wibbly-wobbly, timey-wimey flashback effect here). Dallas, Texas, 1980.

I ride my bicycle after school to my local comic book/movie memorabilia shop. Remember When had opened two years earlier in the little North Dallas town of Farmers Branch and I was among the first to discover this fantastic store and it's treasures of comics old and new, movie posters, lobby cards, TV and movie stills and general sci-fi fandom. In time, owner Larry Herndon promoted me from regular customer to part-time employee. I would bag comics, help customers and generally soak up the atmosphere and educate myself in this wonderful new world. One day while filing movie and TV stills, I came across one that I couldn't identify. It was a black and white photo and featured a man dressed in a Bohemian fashion, with a floppy hat and a large scarf wrapped unendingly around his shoulders. I held up the photo and, I promise, the following conversation took place.

"Hey, Larry, where does this one go?" I enquired.

"That's the Doctor," Larry replied.

"Doctor who?" I asked

"Exactly!" Larry said.

And that was the moment. I had officially been introduced to Tom Baker's Doctor via a single B&W picture. I had to know more about this interesting looking character. Going to the 'D' section of the television stills, I found the folder labeled 'Dr. Who'. I not only found more photos of this Baker fellow but other characters like Sarah Jane, Romana, the Master... and a robot dog named K-9. Flash-forward some months and I'm helping out at a comics/sci-fi convention that *Remember When* was sponsoring. One of my tasks was to help the vendors unload and set up their collectibles that they planned to sell over the weekend. One fellow needed help carrying in something rather large. It was in sections, he informed me, and needed to be assembled at his booth. As we began to carry in the pieces, I was curious as to what it was I had in my hands. They were large panels made of wood and painted blue...

"What is this?" I asked.

"It's a TARDIS," he said

TARDIS. Here was another special moment: my first encounter with Doctor's original companion. An *actual* TARDIS! I learned more about the Doctor and his adventures from this fellow as we continued to set up his booth. Forward again a few months where I'm watching my local PBS station, KERA, Channel 13, in Dallas. I had been watching this station on a regular basis since 1974 when they became the first station in the US to broadcast *Monty Python's Flying Circus*. They gradually added more great British comedies, *The Two Ronnies*, *The Benny Hill Show*, *Are You Being Served*, et al. It was through KERA that I was finally able to get my first view of the Doctor in action.

Fast forward to 2005. I'm much older now and more sophisticated and so, it seems, is the Doctor. The slick new return of Doctor Who slowly but surely made its way into the hearts and minds of a new generation. The "older fans" are mostly on board with the Doctor's return as well.

Now here we are on the eve of the Doctor's fiftieth anniversary. Not only is he popular - again - in Great Britain, but he may be even more popular across the pond thanks to BBC America. Also, thanks to DVD everyone can now relive the Doctor's adventures from Year One and compare "old Doctors" Hartnell and Troughton, Pertwee and Baker (Tom and Colin), Davison and McCoy, and let's not forget McGann!

Whenever I'm with fans, the inevitable question is asked: "Who is your favourite Doctor?" I, of course, always have the perfect answer.

"Yes, he is."

A Whovian in Houston

By Michael Fairview, aged 40, from the USA

I was first introduced to the show Doctor Who by my friend Bryan when he stayed over at my house. We were eight years old and the year was 1981. Normally my parents were very strict with me on when my bedtime was, but on that night, the local Public Broadcasting Station, Channel 8, was showing the 1981 BBC production of *Hitchhiker's Guide to the Galaxy*. After the show, Bryan suggested that we stay up a little while longer to watch his favorite programme. And so, for thirty minutes, I watched this madman with a large blue box, big brown hat, and an impossibly long scarf running around fighting monsters and being brilliant. The next day, we talked about the episode, but quite frankly I didn't understand a lot of it.

I didn't see Doctor Who for two years after that. In fact, it was quite by accident that I found him again. I decided to sneak into the living room after my parents had gone to bed to watch some television. The show was the same, yet different. The same big blue box, the same brilliance... but the madman with the big brown hat and impossibly long scarf had been replaced by another madman with blond hair and a cricket bat. I asked Bryan about it the next day, and he explained to me about the Doctor's regeneration. I was fascinated and hooked.

There was, of course, the matter of my curfew. When I was ten, my bedtime was ten o'clock during the summer months, and eight o'clock during the school year. Back then, Doctor Who came on at 12:30 on Saturday nights - two and a half hours after my curfew. After my parents went to bed, I would sneak to the living room. In my ten year old mind, I pretended that my parents were a pair of Daleks or Cybermen and I had to help the Doctor by watching his adventures on the television. I was on a mission!

So, every Saturday night, I would put on two pairs of socks so that I would be extra quiet and I would take a blanket with me to throw over the television set. I couldn't have the glow of the screen seen from the hallway. Of course, I was eventually caught, and my mother was furious. My father, however, laughed about it.

The next Monday, I found a small black and white television set on the dresser in my room. Next to the set was a note which read: *"As long as you get up to go to worship service with Mom, you can watch Doctor Who in your room"*.

It was a promise I kept until the end of Sylvester McCoy's run in 1989.

Since the show's renewal in 2005, I have watched Doctor Who with my kids, first on the Sci-Fi Network and later on BBC America. To see that Doctor Who has achieved the status it has in America is still amazing to me. When I was younger, I tried to talk to other people about the show. They would roll their eyes and shrug me off. Now, those same people, or their kids at least, wherever they are, might just be Whovians themselves. And that makes me proud to be a Whovian.

Indomitable

By Jimmie Chappell, aged 30, from the USA

It should only be fitting that my first contact with the Doctor was via a large, retro, commercial satellite dish sitting in my front yard back in 1992. I was one of those lonely kids, filled with imagination, running around in the dirt roads and woods near my house dressed up as Batman or pretending to be any other of the myriad of fictional characters I had fallen in love with during my first decade on this planet we call 'Earth'.

When I wasn't saving the world on my own in between school or glued to the set playing Nintendo, I was enjoying the spoils of having a satellite that beamed in countless hours of worlds that were far better than the one I was secluded in for all those years. So when a channel calling itself The Sci-Fi Channel premiered near the end of that year, I was there as if before the channel had even been unveiled. I was hooked and it instantly became one of the anchors of my fantasy storytelling. I was watching *The Incredible Hulk*, *Night Gallery*, anime classics like *Vampire Hunter D* and... wait... what's this coming on?

It was that music. You know it. It's there, playing now like the drumming inside the Master's head. And it always will be. I had never heard anything like it before.

Then, out of the cosmos formed this odd blue box, followed by the face of a man. The wisdom and whimsy was there, tucked beneath the steadfast sternness of that stark stare he had. This was a superhero who didn't take anything but the serious seriously.

And as soon as I had asked the question, apparently so did the title of the show. I was almost too mesmerised by the whole experience, as if it had all been a dream. Soon enough I'd learn when it was coming on and sometimes I knew I'd only have time to watch the opening. One day, a blanket of mountain snow upon our dish was interfering with my spacey music fix. I suited up, walked outside, and - being of childhood stature - resorted to using my father's wood cutting axe to drag across the surface of the dish to clear the snow like an ice scrapper on a windshield. Yes. Foolish looking back, but that theme song was worth it.

Sadly, my time with the Fourth Doctor was to be short lived. I didn't know I would be moving after completing elementary school. New school, new friends and a tighter household budget meant certain luxuries faded for a while, including the vastness of television beamed directly from space. The little time I had with my first Doctor was too mesmerising because, tragically, so much faded from my memory. All I could eventually remember was that curly do, his smile, Sarah Jane's face, jelly babies, that odd, blue box, the running down corridors, and that theme song. They all became these little things that whisked though my nerdy mind from time to time, like ghosts you'd see out of the corner of your eye. Like a song you hear once on the radio that the DJ never identifies, the Doctor was beginning to fade away too rapidly. But a Time Lord doesn't remain lost forever, and he returned to my life towards the end of those unusual middle school years, when Fox began advertising a new TV movie called Doctor Who.

"Wait, what was that?" my newly teenage self said at the advertisement.

Yes, it was Doctor Who. But it was here in America. It was 1996, summer was coming up, and here was an odd televised surprise...

My God. That music. The title. The time vortex. I remember this! I was covered in goose bumps and glued once again, but this time, I was more attentive, learning the rules, the basics, putting together what little I knew while enjoying the ride. I discovered it was called the TARDIS and what it stood for and why it looked the way it did. I discovered regeneration. 13 lives. I even found out where the Doctor kept an extra key, and if I ever spot the TARDIS, I'm going to look there regardless...

But before I knew it, this new adventure was over before it had even began. And you know what happened next, don't you? Cut to 2005 and the Doctor was back in my life. I gave the show an excited look and soon realised that it really wasn't new after all, was it? The rules I knew were still in effect, and somewhere unseen, McGann had become Eccleston. That's one of the many reasons I love Doctor Who. Despite its vast history there is always somewhere for the new fan to come in and not be overwhelmed. A fifty year old show that doesn't discriminate and welcomes all. One has to admire that, even if one isn't a Whovian.

While 2005 had heralded the Doctor's return, it wasn't the best time for me personally. It was the worst year of my life and I hope it stays that way. My life hadn't moved on since graduating high school in 2001, my dreams were going nowhere and my depression deepened with each day. I was lost more than ever and had no companion of my own. Things as wondrous as Doctor Who were losing their magic and even the Ninth Doctor had to go unexpectedly at the end of his first season. I was reminded that things needed to change as he said his unexpected goodbyes to Rose Tyler. I was scared. I had tears in my eyes, unsure of what my own life had in store for me...

Then Tennant appeared in a flash of magnificence and, suddenly, I had forgotten my pain for a moment, alleviated by a Doctor nonetheless. And it was Tennant, a kid who had childhood dreams of his own to become the Doctor, the man he admired more than anyone. He *was* the Doctor and his time in the TARDIS was one in my life that helped keep me going on when I neither had much to cling to nor the will to cling. He helped carry me along, kept me smiling and enthralled and assisted in bringing me to a place where I never thought existed for me. A place as a lover, a best friend, and a soul mate to someone, both spending our lives looking for each other in time and space, all too easily capable of never knowing one another despite nothing but chance keeping us apart. The Doctor took me in the TARDIS all the way to 27th May 2009 when a beautiful girl named Ren introduced herself to me digitally, eventually leading to our first date. I had at last found my companion.

I know that if I ever met David Tennant, I would lose it and cry. Imagine that - a 6'2" big, burly man with a robust beard bawling uncontrollably. But that would occur if I ever met him. He has brought so much joy and wisdom into my life. He kept me going when I thought I was done and I thank him from the very bottom of my heart for that, for being exactly where I needed him, exactly *when* I needed him. Maybe he really is the Doctor.

Time and love. That's what this is all about, isn't it? The two things that seem infinite yet we all struggle to find enough of. I think that's the best part about Doctor Who. We imagine such fantastic worlds, the things that inhabit them, and the events that occur. And in that impossible moment in time, we all share a real love. For that moment in time, be it film or the written word, visual or audible, we're not strangers. We're a family loving something so much, believing in it hard enough that it's real. Quoting and referencing it, reliving it endlessly, and taking inspiration from it on a daily basis, we reach a point where no force on Earth can shake our faith in it, not even in our darkest of moments...

Wanna watch some Doctor Who?

The Greatest Show

By David W. Robinson, aged 42, from New York, USA

Doctor Who is the greatest show in the history of television. It's a literary chameleon. It can tell its tale on any planet in the universe and at any point in time. An unlimited scope. The concept of regeneration, introduced at the start of the fourth season and not even fully explained until the third time it happened, gives the show an unlimited longevity. I expect it to run for hundreds of years into the future, which is something I believed even before it went off the air in 1989. Now it seems absolutely and inevitably possible that it will.

I know that officially the BBC labels it a children's television show, but the first time I saw it, aged 8, I must say I didn't like it at all. I found it all rather confusing and boring. I was born in 1970 in New York where, during the late 70s, the first few Tom Baker seasons were airing locally on WWOR, Channel 9, as well as on local PBS station WNET, Channel 13. I now know that the first serial I saw was *The Ark in Space*, in which there is a lot of walking around on a white walled circular space station and the monster seems to be just a green blob. I am lacking a better reason for my negative reaction to the show when I was younger...

I rediscovered Doctor Who during the summer of 1984. I was 13 years old and just about to start 9th grade at a new high school. One Saturday night I was stuck at home with nothing good to watch on TV. I was scanning through the TV guide when I noticed the New Jersey Network had a listing for Doctor Who at 9pm. To watch it I had to first manually tune into the channel by using a wheel, guessing which channel was number 50. I eventually came upon it and the first image I saw was the view out of the window of a spaceship. The ship soon gets stuck in a time loop and I was quickly sucked into the plot of the story. It was the 'movie version' of *The Armageddon Factor* and I found myself eagerly and impatiently awaiting next week's showing. That happened to be the 'movie version' of *Destiny of the Daleks*, which not only introduced me to the Daleks and Davros, but also to the concept of a Time Lord's regeneration. It was here that I also got my first glimpse of the show's greatest recruiting tool - the opening theme. That music has been instantly beloved by all my new fan converts and I would always play the episodic versions of stories to them specifically to increase the number of times we would hear the song. We never, ever fast-forwarded through it. It has evolved so much over the years but always remains haunting and special.

And so the weeks rolled by and soon I saw Tom Baker regenerate into Peter Davison, whose first few stories quickly drew me in. It was around this time I discovered Doctor Who Magazine in a comic book shop a few blocks from my house and I started going to Doctor Who conventions in early 1985. During my very first one I was told that we were the lucky ones who would get to see the new Sixth Doctor Season 22 opener *Attack of the Cybermen* on a big screen in the hotel theatre. I've since had may more great convention moments, including my mother and brothers and I being invited to share drinks with Matthew Waterhouse (Fourth and Fifth Doctor companion Adric) who turned out to be really personable and fun. A couple of years later I shared an elevator ride with Seventh Doctor Sylvester McCoy who was incredibly gracious. The 1980s were a truly magical time for me.

Arabian Nights

By Christopher Hawton, aged 34, from the UK

I'm British and I'm writing this while listening to cricket commentary in Hampshire. Just outside my window, there's some crown green bowling going on. It's all very British or, in fact, English. My daily commute takes me right past where that comedy Frenchman Taltalian picks up Liz Shaw as she is trying to hitch a lift to safety in *The Ambassadors of Death*. However, I didn't become a fan here.

When I was in single figures, I was living in Abu Dhabi, an island city off the coast of the United Arab Emirates. The only English-language programming we had were the 80s action shows *The A-Team* and *Knight Rider*. At that time Abu Dhabi TV didn't go in much for science fiction for whatever reason, but then one day I stumbled across this mad creepy programme - an omnibus edition of *Planet of Evil*. My brother was freaked out by the anti-matter monster, particularly when it took over Sorenson. As for me, I was gripped. I don't actually remember my first impression of the Doctor as much as the brilliant horrors lurking on the planet Zeta Minor, which was so unlike anything I'd seen before. My Mum then mentioned that we had a Doctor Who video, *The Five Doctors*, and that was me sold -for life, as it's turned out - and the Doctor has been a regular part of my life ever since.

For my eighth birthday party we rented out a slightly dodgy recorded-off-TV copy of *Timelash* from our local video store (copyright law wasn't particularly vigorously forced in those parts in the 80s!). Quite what my mates made of it I don't know, but I loved it. As a result I ended up churning out lots of fan fiction at school. One slightly disturbing story revealed how the Sixth Doctor acquired Peri at a robot market. Maybe it was my child mind's way of trying to excuse some of the excesses of Colin's Doctor's behaviour...

While my somewhat awkward teenage self would identify with football teams and bands, my primary interest would still be the Doctor. I had Doctor Who Magazine on subscription and ripping open the bag was always a highlight of the month. These were my people. And then, at university, I turned slightly away from the show. Looking back, I reckon it was an urge to be accepted. As the McGann wilderness wore on into the late 90s, my Doctor Who Magazine subscription lapsed and I would severely downplay my knowledge of the show. Sure I watched *The Curse of Fatal Death* sketch for Comic Relief, but I knew my Doctor Who was long dead and, besides, what else would a household of somewhat socially awkward science students do on a Friday night but watch slightly disappointing comedy...?

Then, one Christmas, I was being introduced to my parents' new neighbour, a long-retired lighting technician. We spoke in depth about Kubrick and Lean over cheese and wine. I admired his BAFTA award up on the mantelpiece. And then I asked - whispered, more like - whether he had ever worked on Doctor Who. I think, apologetic to the last, I prefaced it with "I'm sorry, but I've got to ask..."

And guess what? He had. He had worked on the show from *An Unearthly Child* through to *Marco Polo*, and so began a series of chats whenever I was down. Discussions over cheese and wine about what Hartnell and Troughton were like and how brave and driven Verity Lambert was. As the new series was announced and entered production, he dropped a second bombshell. His daughter-in-law was working on the costumes and one costume in particular: the new Doctor's costume.

Today, I still find it weird that the show is no longer just a cult thing and deep down I still expect it to fade away again. The next time it takes a leave of absence, though, as Russell T Davies has pointed out, it will return again in time and that thought is an amazing one given how things once were. Who would have predicted back in 1993 that, twenty years down the line, the identity of the next Doctor would be simulcast live around the world?

It's amazing stuff, this little show.

From One Zygon to Another

By Guy Newmountain, aged 47, from the UK

My first memory of Doctor Who occurred at school around a year or two before I actually saw the show for the first time. It was 1971 and we were living in London. I was five years old, in those days we were "bussed" to somewhere else for school dinner and one of the other kids on my table asked, in a confidential, hushed, almost reverent-yet-fearful tone, "Did you see Doctor Who?"

At that age I didn't even understand what was being discussed, but the buzz of excitement that the topic generated among my classmates was something that could not fail to leave an impression.

Fast forward a year to 1972. We had moved to Bucklebury, a little village in the Berkshire countryside which is mentioned, believe it or not, in Tolkien's *Lord of the Rings*. Post-Christmas lethargy prevailed and my exhausted mother was trying to find something to interest her two little boys. I clearly remember her announcing, as she flicked through the *Radio Times*, that a new programme was beginning that afternoon which I might like. "It's full of monsters," she said. That did the trick.

Even the title sequence was scary. Those hypnotic, flickering flames and the twisting spirals of the time vortex. Coupled with Delia Derbyshire's classic version of Ron Grainer's alien theme music, none of us had any idea how utterly compelling and far-reaching the impact of seeing the programme for the first time would be. It was like nothing I had ever seen before. My little brother found the show too scary, however, and so after a couple of episodes I was left watching alone each Saturday. Although half of it was gobbledygook to me, the thought of missing my favourite programme was a far greater source of anxiety than any of the monsters.

Asking for the TV to be put on way before time, switching out the lights and drawing the curtains was all part of the ritual to maximize that delicious feeling of fear. When the *Radio Times* came through the door each Tuesday, I literally could not wait to reach the Saturday page. Frank Bellamy's (and later Peter Brookes') dramatic illustrations accompanying the weekly episode listings offered a tantalising clue about the following instalment. For me, and no doubt a legions of others, Doctor Who *was* the weekend. When it was over it felt as if the whole weekend was over. It was literally all I cared about.

And then, the shock announcement from my mother that the Doctor was going to "change his face". She had heard it on the radio - the word "regenerate" had not even been coined at that time. Jon Pertwee - leaving? How could anyone else come even close? He was the only Doctor I had ever known and suddenly, on 8th June 1974, there he was, lying broken on the laboratory floor in *Planet of the Spiders*, transforming into... who was this impostor? He looked useless!

When the TV show eventually returned, aside from the new title sequence featuring a haunting shot of Tom Baker, I was distinctly unimpressed and actually very wary of the newcomer. It took until midway through *The Sontaran Experiment* for him to finally eclipse Jon Pertwee and win me over. My brother and I wrote letters to the Doctor and Tom Baker responded with a pair of signed black and white photo postcards and a personal letter (how I wish I still had it!) mentioning the upcoming Loch Ness Monster. And then it was announced that the Doctor himself would be appearing - LIVE! - at what I believe was some sort of charity fundraising day in Reading. I could not sleep, enlisting the help of my little brother to help me colour in a huge felt-tip Dalek drawing for Tom Baker to sign...

The big day arrived and the venue was packed with children. All the preliminary acts have long since been forgotten, but finally, after what seemed like an eternity, the theme music began blaring out, the circular stage started rotating clockwise and there was the Doctor himself, in full previous Season 12 costume. The scarf, the hat, the wine coloured jacket. Our eyes were like saucers. He was the tallest person I had ever seen. I vaguely recall Tom making a speech about the good cause - Barnardo's, I think - and then he was virtually mobbed by all of us pushing and jostling for signings.

"Oh, that's a very good one!" he said as he wrote on my Dalek picture in blue biro (a valuable autograph my innocent nine year old self would later that day render entirely worthless by going over it in chunky red felt-tip to make it stand out!). There he was, babies being put in his arms, kissing them like a politician, and, as we were driven away, I spotted him through the windscreen, now on the building's roof and still surrounded by crazed fans. What a memory that is. The Doctor, the ultimate hero.

Even before the days of the Doctor Who Appreciation Society, at the age of ten, I ran a Doctor Who fan club in my primary school at lunchtimes. I once bet a lad 50p that I could build a full-size Dalek and he bet I would never complete it. Suffice to say, he won. My art teacher sat on the fibreglass head mould as it was setting, leaving the shape of her bottom forever indented in it. Disillusioned, I never got further than its head and neck!

Of all the companions, Sarah Jane's exit in *The Hand of Fear* was a really major thing. I tried to pretend that it wasn't, but that freeze frame where she is caught in mid-walk at the end still leaves a lump in my throat. I can't tell you how sad and shocked I was to wake up and hear the news that the beautiful Elisabeth Sladen had passed away. I met Elisabeth twice - the first time was long before the series had returned at the opening of a Forbidden Planet shop in London. I was quite in awe ('a little tongue-tied' as I put it - she was still so breathtakingly attractive!) but she nevertheless took time to engage each and every visitor. Elisabeth Sladen, the Doctor's best friend. The beautiful, utterly irreplaceable, Sarah Jane Smith.

Over the years I have experienced first-hand the extraordinary power that Doctor Who has to reunite lives. In my early thirties, nearing the end of a six month desktop publishing course amid a group of other trainees, I started testing out Macromedia Freehand software by drawing, predictably, a Dalek. Glancing over at my Mac, a new friend of mine remarked, "You know, I used to know someone years ago who drew Daleks all the time. How can you do all that from memory? Have you always lived in Leicester?" Not really focusing, I nodded absentmindedly, then murmured as an afterthought, "Well, I did live in a tiny country village when I was little. Bucklebury." And she froze. It only turned out we had been in the same class there together - I was that little boy she had remembered, twenty-five years earlier, who was always drawing Daleks! Had I not done so there and then, we would never have known we were so closely linked. And it is key, priceless events like that which just make Doctor Who the most wonderful phenomenon. It is a truly magical and enduring part of my life.

Lost and Found

By Heather Leonard, aged 35, from the USA

I grew up watching science fiction with my Dad. My earliest memories involved sitting in his lap watching *Star Trek*, *Buck Rogers*, and *Battlestar Galactica*, but I didn't discover Doctor Who until I was in high school in the mid 90s. Our local public television station aired the series in the wee hours of Saturday and Sunday mornings. I often passed out from of sheer exhaustion because of the time, while visions of jelly babies danced in my head. I was a drama geek at school and my friends and I often got together to watch the show, which we all loved for its fun plots. We were a tiny group of Whovians in a country where it seemed that most people had never even heard of Doctor Who.

I think my exposure to Doctor Who largely influenced my decision to study Drama in college. Right after I graduated from high school, I joined a college-based theatre company as an actor and technical grunt. One day, Mike, the tech director, asked me to go upstairs to the scenery attic to locate some Greek columns he needed for an upcoming show. The scenery attic was enormous, dirty, and poorly lit. One bare, 40-watt bulb at the top of the stairs was all the place had for illumination, so sojourns to the attic always involved a flashlight. It was easy to feel like you were in a bad horror flick or an episode of *Scooby Doo* up there. That day, by the light of the fading flashlight beam, I nearly fell over in surprise at what I'd found.

A dusty old TARDIS.

It was a perfect replica, just sitting there in the corner as if the Doctor himself had parked it and run off to join the theatre company (I wouldn't put that past him, would you?). I'm sure I was grinning like an idiot when I touched the magnificent blue box, nudged the door open, and stepped in. Sadly, though, it wasn't bigger on the inside and contained no renegade Time Lords. The flashlight chose to die then, which meant I had to navigate my way back to the stairs in the dark. The scene that followed probably went something like this:

Heather: *(Running into the workshop, covered in dust)* Mike!

Mike: Did you find the columns?

Heather: No, but I found a TARDIS! Why do we have a TARDIS?

Mike: A what?

Heather: From Doctor Who? You know, the British TV show about a guy who travels through time and space in a blue police box?

Mike: I have no idea what you're talking about.

It was a lost and found TARDIS. The mystery went unsolved for several weeks but it turns out that the battered old TARDIS had been used in a musical review in the mid 80s. It had been shoved in the attic and left to rot. I don't know anything about the production, but the company members and I had a good old time imagining our own songs. My favourite was our parody of *Do You Hear the People Sing?* from *Les Misérables...*

"Do you hear the Time Lords sing? Singing the songs of Gallifrey? It is the music of a people who have mastered time and space..."

You know, I think that my life is a little like that lost and found TARDIS that I discovered in the dusty old theatre attic so many years ago. The ship was lost and forgotten, much like my original dream of a career in theatre and film. The TARDIS was eventually found, though, much to the delight of the company members who loved it so much. My dream was rediscovered after turning back to science fiction, helping me to find the courage to face down the darkness that had made me lose that dream in the first place. I'm going back to doing something I love and Doctor Who was an influence in helping me to finally make that decision.

We are not Time Lords. We can't regenerate. We only have one shot at life and it's far too short to sit around and be unhappy all the time when there's so many amazing adventures out there. If there's anything I've learned from Doctor Who, it's that in order to follow your dreams, you have to jump in feet first and you can't be afraid.

Oh, and yelling and screaming probably helps, too!

The Lost Autograph

By Richard Trefla, aged 40, from the UK

I can't remember when I first watched Doctor Who. I have two brothers who are both much older than me, so I guess I must have simply been there while they were watching it. It must have been during the reign of Tom Baker. My memory of my early years is fairly vague and patchy all over, really, but one memory I do have branded into my brain is of seeing the Doctor. It is one of my claims to fame. I have actually met the mighty Tom Baker!

There was a fate at my brothers' school and it was opened by Mr Baker himself. I don't remember anything else about the day, except trying to squeeze through the legs of people much taller than me - I was probably only five or six years old at the time - and thrusting a programme at him as soon I had got to the front. I was close enough to touch him. I walked round on cloud nine for the rest of the day.

All I need now is a time machine to go back and find the programme with his autograph on it...

The Doctor and his Fans

By Christine Grit, aged 47, from the Netherlands

I've enjoyed watching Doctor Who since I was 8 or 9. At that time, the show was not only broadcast via the BBC in the UK, but also on Dutch television. At home it was shown on Fridays and I recall always being very excited whenever the programme was on. Luckily for us, we lived in the South West of the country so we could also watch the show on the BBC. For a short period it was a real weekend treat, being able to watch the show both on Fridays and Saturdays. However, the Dutch broadcaster stopped quite abruptly after receiving complaints about children getting nightmares. Then, for as long as we remained living in the South West, we could still watch the show on the BBC. And then we moved to the North and there was no BBC available anymore.

As long as we lived in the South West, however, the show was something my brother and I really looked forward to, even if it sometimes scared us. I remember being freaked out by the Cybermats in *Revenge of the Cybermen*, though not by the Cybermen themselves.

While I was attending high school in the early 80s, Doctor Who finally returned to Dutch television screens. You can perhaps imagine my surprise in finding out that the funny guy with the scarf was not present at all, just some other bloke wearing the kind of suit I expected posh students to wear. He seemed to be rather kind, but also rather timid, and had somehow taken the place of my eccentric humorous original. As it happened, I had never even heard of regeneration. I presumed that with Doctor Who the same things happened as in soap series, with the writing out of characters, and writing new ones in whenever appropriate. Strangely though, this new lead was still called 'the Doctor', while the TARDIS was also still a central part of the programme. Didn't the TARDIS belong to the real Doctor? Shouldn't he be the guy with the big smile and the absurdly long scarf?

Today, I currently consider myself to be a fan of both the Classic and New series. I've paid visits to the Doctor Who Experience and will also visit conventions if at all possible. I'll dress up as a Dalek whenever appropriate. I currently participate in certain blogs and forums on the web and I follow fellow fans on Facebook and Twitter. It's so much fun watching and reading about your favourite show!

The Saga of Lindalee Rose
By Steve Czarnecki, aged 40, from the USA

My name is Steve and I am a Doctor Who fan. I guess that statement makes it sound like I'm at a Time Lord's Anonymous meeting, but I have been a committed Whovian since the mid 70S. Born in South Florida, it was around 5 or 6 years old that I discovered rebroadcasts of the BBC's hit show on our local PBS station. I was intrigued and fascinated by the colourful character who went by the simple name of "The Doctor", being wonderfully portrayed during those broadcasts by Tom Baker. Doctor Who helped lay the foundations for my love of science fiction for decades to come by exposing me to space, time, aliens, robots and otherworldly adventures. It was enough to feed my already overly imaginative childhood.

Along with many others, I'm sure, I was excited to see the return of the series in 2005 on BBC America. The reboot brought a fresh new approach geared for a new generation and yet it still managed to connect with its classic fan base built over the span of 40 years.My oldest daughter, Lindalee Rose, used to curl up with my wife and I on our couch during the David Tennant era and it was just before her 2nd birthday in April 2010 that *The Eleventh Hour* premiered. I recall her being drawn to the screen with absolute fascination watching Amelia Pond interacting with the new Doctor. There was something about little Amy interacting with an overly excited grown up that hooked my daughter's attention. Though she may not have fully understood the premise of the show, from then on watching Doctor Who with her daddy became a weekly ritual.

On Labour Day weekend of 2012, the first episode of the seventh season, *Asylum of the Daleks*, premiered and Lindalee and I were planted on the couch watching intently. Watching my all-time favourite Doctor Who enemies - the Daleks - giving the Doctor, Amy and Rory a run for their money was very intriguing not only for me, but Lindalee as well. Watching the episode, she would interject with questions from time to time and I was more than happy to explain what was happening so she could fully enjoy the show. When it was over, my wife Rebekah simply asked Lindalee how the show was and what she thought of it. To our complete surprise, for the next few minutes, Lindalee gave my wife and I an almost perfect recap of the show from start to finish. We heard everything from "the Doctor being captured by the big Daddy Dalek" to "the planet exploding!"

We were stunned. Her energy, enthusiasm, recollection and delivery of the episode had us speechless. She not only loved the show, but she *understood* it. To her credit, my wife looked at me and said, "You should record this." I immediately grabbed my video camera, sat Lindalee down on a chair and asked her to tell us again all about the episode and what she thought about it. Holding onto one of my toy Daleks and a Sonic Screwdriver, she was more than happy to oblige. And so it began... Lindalee's first "Doctor Who Review".

In addition to my daily job, I am also the creator and producer of an online entertainment website called *BeyondTheMarquee.com*. Always looking for new features and sometimes just something to post for daily content, I decided to post the video of my daughter on the site. After a slight edit and polish of the footage complete with credits and appropriate music, Lindalee's first review was released on Monday 4th September 2012. Not thinking too much of it, I sent the link to a few Doctor Who fan sites and entertainment news blogs as well. A few days later, I got an email from a friend saying that Doctor Who showrunner, Steven Moffat, just tweeted Lindalee's review link out to his 400,000+ Twitter followers. Before we knew it, *Lindalee's Doctor Who Review* had jumped from 100 views to over 10,000 in less than 24 hours. By the end of that weekend, it had surpassed over 30,000 hits. As a result, Lindalee was being reposted on Doctor Who and sci-fi websites all around the world. For my wife and I, the attention was truly unexpected and the reception our daughter received was positive and supportive. Lindalee said she enjoyed doing the video and was up for doing more, and we continue producing them to this day.

Over the next few months, *Lindalee's Doctor Who Review* continued to pull in viewers and brought with them tons of comments from fans all over the globe who had connected with Lindalee's reviews in one way or another. Some agreed with her innocent takes on the complex dramas that unfolded in the episodes while others chuckled at her impersonations of Matt Smith. It was amazing to see how one little girl could reach out and bring so many Whovians together. With the need for a bit more sparkle, the reviews went through some improvements and soon found Lindalee arriving on her own set in a custom-built TARDIS.

Lindalee's first big public VIP appearance occurred at the Gallifrey One convention in Los Angeles, California in the spring of 2013. It was there she witnessed creative costumes, fellow Whovians and saw more Doctor Who toy products then she could have ever imagined. In between talking to fans on camera, she also got to interview some of the special guest attendees including Sylvester McCoy (the Seventh Doctor), Freema Agyeman (the Tenth Doctor's companion Martha Jones) and Nick Briggs (the voice of the Daleks). The highlight for her, as well as me, occurred when Lindalee was invited on stage with Freema during her Q&A. With enthusiasm and confidence, Lindalee received a sea of applause and took a seat next to her new friend, Freema. A Doctor Who 'knock knock' joke and a question about a bathroom on the TARDIS had the 3,000+ attendees in the auditorium rolling with laughter. At that moment, I realised a full sense of pride and accomplishment as a father and I was swelling with emotion and fighting back happy tears. In five short months, a simple idea of recording my daughter's response to a favourite show of mine had brought about a connection to Doctor Who we could have never imagined.

As long as Lindalee enjoys watching and reviewing Doctor Who, we will continue creating entertaining content for the fans. With the support of the BBC, fans from around the world, and most importantly her family and friends, we'll be ready to shout "Geronimo!" if and when the time comes. In the meantime, we're still pinching ourselves to make sure it's not all a dream!

My Doctor is Unbound

By Michael Nixon, aged 24, from the USA

My first proper episode of Doctor Who was the last five minutes of *Logopolis* which feature possibly the strangest regeneration in the series. What I didn't know at the time was that the standard regenerations to that date had featured a simple cross-fade from one face to the other. But the regeneration of Tom Baker into Pater Davison added a strange new element to the transition: The Watcher. What was the young, impressionable me supposed to make of the strange, white-garbed fellow with the gooey face who walked into the chest of the curly-haired old Doctor, just before he turned into the mousey-haired younger new Doctor? The alien nature of the Doctor was clear, and so was the strangeness of the regenerative process. But, foremost in my head was a simple question. What was the deal with that chalky-faced Watcher chap?

I watched the whole run of episodes on my PBS station, from *Logopolis* to *Survival* with nary a hint of evidence. While I quickly became hooked on the show, my interest in that strange extra un-Doctor never faded. This wasn't helped by the addition of the sinister Valeyard, a distillation of the Doctor's dark side and a potential future incarnation given life by the Time Lords. There were other Doctors beyond the "official" ones, and apocrypha is where I eat.

Even when the PBS reruns rolled over to the classic Hartnell episodes, my curiosity about these strange Other Doctors was left unchecked. Eventually, I circled back around to the Tom Baker serial *The Brain of Morbius* which would add to my curiosity in the form of a few extra faces tacked on before Hartnell "They're just Morbius," shouted the fans. They never say that in the episode," replied me.

And, as my pre-New Series fandom grew, new faces would be added to the pile of unofficial Doctors. It would be another extra face, featured in *Scream of the Shalka* (that sadly-aborted webcast featuring future Doctor Who villain Richard E. Grant as the Doctor, future Master Sir Derek Jacobi as a different Master, and future Whovian action-queen Sophie Okenodo as companion Alison) that would be my next weird alternative. I watched those webisodes eagerly, enjoying every one. I still own the novelization - two copies, actually, due to a shipping error - and I even read the online-only short story featuring a new Ninth Doctor, an official Doctor whose fresh adventures I could enjoy.

But, sadly, some bloke in a leather jacket was quickly announced as the true successor to the Doctor Who title just weeks into my newfound love, crushing my rechristened Shalka Doctor into obscurity. A Ninth Doctor who never was.

This only fuelled my interest in the odd Doctors out. The esoteric parts of Doctor Who became the corners I loved. The Doctors who never were. Unbound Doctors, Doctors afflicted with the deadly Curse of Fatal Death, along with Watchers, Valeyards, Merlins, and Others.

I loved - and still love - the fan theories. The weird Doctors who can't exist. The sideways Doctors in continuity cul-de-sacs. One of my more well read novels is *The Infinity Doctors*, with its undefined and anti-continuity Doctor, a Doctor I can mentally re-define every time I read him.

So, you can have your Tennant, you can have your Smith, you can have your Baker... either one. Here's to the strange ones, the rebels, the distant dreams. Here's to the Doctors on the edge. Here's to the Doctors who defy the very borders of continuity. Here's to the Doctors who never were and yet always have been.

My Doctor is unbound.

A Reformed Whovian
By Rebecca, aged 33, from the US

My first memory of Doctor Who is of Tom Baker's scarf from when I was a little kid. Ironically, Tom Baker's Doctor was the only one my father (who is a sc-ifi fan) ever watched - I think my memory comes from watching it with him, or at least being in the room while it was on.

Fast forward to 2005, when I was 25 years old. By this point I have already become an anglophile and BBC America was my favourite channel. One day, I came to it and there was the Doctor and Rose at the end of the world. I watched the whole episode and fell totally in love with Doctor Who - fully and consciously this time. So I made sure and never missed an episode of the Ninth Doctor. I adored Christoper Eccelston and was devastated to hear he was leaving. I watched up to the end of his season and, as any Whovian understands: "the next Doctor is NOT my Doctor!" I did quit watching the show, unfortunately. I just couldn't imagine anyone else in that role.

Fast forward again to 2013, ironically the 50th year of Doctor Who, and I make a friend at work who is a Whovian - and over the years, of course, I heard all about how wonderful and amazing and beautiful David Tennant was, and I even remember hearing about his departure and Matt Smith being chosen as the Eleventh. I finally decide that it's time to catch up. Enough time has passed that I've gotten over Eccelston leaving.

So over the course of the next two or so weeks, I watch all of Tennant's episodes and all of Smith's episodes on *Netflix* (and season seven on *Amazon*) and fall in love all over again. Words will never describe how much I still love the show and how much I love both Tennant and Smith. Every Whovian always has "their" Doctor - but I have two! The last two. Ten and Eleven. I can literally now not choose between them.

I then decided to watch all the Classic Doctor Who on *Netflix* (which unfortunately isn't ALL of the Classic Who - just what has been saved I guess, but it's better then nothing) and then I knew why I remembered Tom Baker so much. He's just an unforgettable Doctor and rightly is many people's favorite.

The Doctor has been getting me through a rough time. He is always there and he always makes me laugh, and yes, cry. He teaches us so much about life and love, and now I don't know how I went so long without him. I'm happy to have him back!

Of Scarves and Screwdrivers

By Shawn M. Becker, aged 43, from Illinois, USA

"Would you like a jelly baby?"

He came into my life in 1982 with the tip of a floppy hat and the wave of a twelve foot scarf. He was battling Sutekh and his mummies with his friend Sarah Jane and I had no idea what I had paused to watch on our local PBS station.

I came back for more, mostly for the interesting stories, but also for the Doctor. Tom Baker - my Doctor. His booming, British accent accompanied by the occasional boisterous laugh and the toothy grin that seemed to welcome you to his adventures had me hooked. Add in the danger his female companions seem to discover every episode and a tin, robotic dog and I was a Whovian.

By the age of thirteen, I was running around in the hot July sun wearing a corduroy dinner jacket and a 6ft crocheted scarf . Not to act out any Doctor Who storylines, but just to dress like Tom and his Doctor! At this point, I knew all there was to know about the fourth Doctor - yes, I knew there were Doctors before (in the old days), but I was quite content watching the reruns on PBS from part one of *Robot* to part four of *The Horns of Nimon*.

Shock and awe came to me in the guise of John Nathan-Turner.

"It is the end, but the moment has been prepared for."

With those words, my Doctor, Tom Baker, regenerated into Peter Davison... and I had mixed feelings. He was not Tom. And I screamed when he unraveled the scarf I so desperately wanted to own. But, here was a younger man, a younger Doctor, with hair the style and color of my own. Perhaps he and his younger crew weren't so bad after all? The ironic part was that out here in the corn and soybean fields of Illinois - the Davison era was during the years of 1983 to 1985 - clearly long after Peter had left the part in Great Britain.

It was during the Davison era that the show became something more powerful to me. I did not have a pleasant family life. My dysfunctional family consisted of two alcoholic parents that slowly ripped apart any normalcy we could have had. My entry into high school was marred by bullying and the lack of any nearby friends. During the warm months, I could meet up with the neighborhood kids (who went to a different school), but the winter months were hell.

All I had was the Doctor. This new Time Lord had young companions, Adric, Nyssa, and Tegan and the four of them seemed to join as a family. Peter Davison's portrayal was something I desperately craved for my own existence, that nurturing, caring adult who would do everything he could to keep you out of trouble. I wanted to be one of the TARDIS companions. I wanted to be friends with Adric, I had a crush on Nyssa, I wanted to argue with Tegan, and I wanted to show Turlough how wrong he was about the Doctor...

Time passed. The show was canceled. America tried to resurrect it with a fantastic portrayal by Paul McGann. It was just not meant to be. Even when the rumours started with a new BBC production of Doctor Who in 2005, I wasn't thrilled with Christopher Eccleston's version. It was too flashy - he tried too hard to be kooky. Everything about the show screamed *"forget the past...this is the new Who!"*

And then, one day, I happen to catch a rerun of a Christmas episode where the Doctor has regenerated. David Tennant appeared, and his interpretation - as well as the writers - made me pause. *"New teeth...that's weird."*

Since then, I have become a rabid fan once more. And to a British television show that saved a Middle American teenager from turning to abusive forms of escape, I salute the iconic Doctor Who. May the Doctor forever travel the winds of time, may his scarf be forever long and may his sonic screwdrivers illuminate the shadows around us. Happy 50th anniversary, Doctor!

Time Travel the Easy Way
By Mark Aldridge, aged 44, from the UK

November 1989 and the world seems just a little duller than before. The novelty of studying in a new city is wearing thin, as is the lack of money. Sure, I'm enjoying my course, the company of my girlfriend and the buzz of the Student Union, but something is missing. Shaking myself out of my torpor I head into town to mooch about before the evening's entertainment. Lashed by rain I take refuge in the nearest music store, a siren call pulling me towards one particular corner, inhabited by people who look, perhaps, a little like me. My hand reaches out and grabs a VHS case, its cover depicting a foetus-like creature alongside the strangely familiar face of a wild-eyed, wild-haired man. All nostalgia bells ring at once. In my hands is my childhood favourite, *Terror of the Zygons*.

The desire to get home and view my acquisition overrides any interest in the evening's activities. Upon arrival I wrestle the box from its shrink-wrap, remove the cassette and fumble it into the top-loader of the VCR. After hitting play, and adjusting the tracking control, I sit down for the viewing. Before enjoyment, however, comes trepidation. Does memory cheat? Will it look cheap? Will I be disappointed? In a few moments I have my answers: *"maybe a little"*, *"extremely"*, and *"definitely not"*.

I am experiencing feelings long forgotten. This is not a TV show, but a time machine, transporting me back to the late summer of 1975. The Doctor, Harry, Sarah and, of course, the Brigadier captivate me all over again and I know that this is a world to which I will escape with regularity. Too many things ebb away post-childhood: the sense of wonder, the unfettered imagination and the outlook untainted by cynicism. I have recaptured the magic that I didn't know I had lost and I want to keep hold of it. I watch that cassette at least half a dozen times over the following week. Tom Baker's performance is electrifying. Funny, knowledgeable, dependable and maybe even a little scary in places. He is so much better than I remember and the show is so much more than I had hoped for.

March 2005, and maybe it's time to stop looking back, my collection of DVDs is languishing in a dark corner. Then, a series of revelations. Effervescent Eccleston, the Moxx of Balhoon, creepy children in gas masks... The time machine has reactivated, dragging me into a present where sophisticated storylines and sky high production values captivate a whole new generation. I stand shoulder to shoulder with work colleagues, all eager to discuss the latest developments.

May 2013 and the Doctor is now a bandy-legged young man with a penchant for bow ties. He is also, perhaps, the best ever. Diana Rigg is pitch-perfect as a boo-hiss villain and Neil Gaiman - yes, *Neil Gaiman!* - is writing for the show. In a breathless finale the Doctor crosses his own time stream, fusing the best of past and present, while the final moments leave me impatient for an unbearably exciting future.

The time machine is fully functional and I will always be along for the ride.

1979: A TARDIS Odyssey
By Rachel Redhead, aged 40, from Durham, UK

1979 has a bouquet certainly, though it's more a table wine, but I'm getting a month ahead of myself here. Saturday 1st September was the day I fell in love with Doctor Who. It was love at first sight, I was six years old and thought I knew it all. The Doctor and Romana flew through time and space in a blue police box having marvellous adventures. How could a girl like me resist our heroes doing battle with the Daleks?

I suppose it was the unknown that kept me interested, you never knew where the Doctor, Romana and K-9 would turn up next, or what kind of adventure they would have when they got there. From the bleak techno-future of Destiny of the Daleks to the suave chic of Paris and the isolated jungle menace of Chloris, it was the (apparent) death of K-9 at the end of Part 1 of *The Creature from the Pit* that proved too shocking for me and I stopped watching the show out of sheer terror and sadness that the beloved robot dog had died....

It wasn't until 31st January 1981 that I dared to watch the show again and much had changed. Romana had gone and there was a new character travelling with the Doctor, a boy seemingly just a few years older than myself who seemed daring and cheeky and intelligent. His name was Adric and I immediately felt some sort of identification with him as he was closer to my age than the Doctor was.

Over the years following this I've watched all the stories available to watch as well as the 'orphan episodes', acquainted myself with all the Doctors and got a handle on the show's mythology. I've seen Doctors come and go and enjoyed them all for who they were and never judged them or thought they should do anything differently or compare them to other Doctors and the actors who have played them. Yes I have my favourites, I really like the 2nd, 6th, 10th and 11th Doctors, but I don't dislike the others at all.

It's not just the telly show either, I spent much of the 1990s reading all the original novels I could get my hands on, following the adventures of the first eight Doctors on the written page. Then came the audios, adding an extra layer to the experience as well as some new friends of the Doctor and even some alternate versions of the Doctor from other dimensions.

So, what does Doctor Who mean to me? It's been a huge part of my life, more so than anything else. Other interests have come and gone but the Doctor's always been there for me, and hopefully he always will be.

(Re)generation to (Re)generation
By Susan Willetts, aged 39, from Birmingham, UK

I remember way back to being a very little girl, going round for family tea at my nannies on Saturdays. After tea, while the grown ups tidied away and washed up, my Uncle and I would watch Doctor Who, all cosy in the dark of the living room.

I loved Tom Baker with his kindness, jelly babies and K-9. I remember seeing *Worzel Gummidge* being the Doctor before him but I hadn't liked it, I thought he was creepy. But Tom captured my heart and soul and I was hooked. I recall being really sad when Tom's Doctor fell and died, and that the vet man from *All Creatures Great and Small* became the Doctor. How could the Doctor be the vet man!?

This is when I started watching the re-runs of the older Doctors. I saw the First Doctor and thought the stories were good but his incarnation was a little grumpy. I liked the Second Doctor, however. He was strange looking in his big bear coat, but he was much funnier and kinder.

When Colin Baker took over, that shook me. Suddenly the Doctor was scary and out of control. It made for uneasy watching, seeing him throttle poor Peri, and then the press started mentioning that the show's viewer numbers were falling. I felt sad, just because the Doctor was 'not quite right' it didn't mean he wasn't our Doctor and that we should give up on him. He got better, though still loud and out spoken.

The Trial of a Time Lord episodes were fantastic, just as good as some of the old stories, and so my faith was restored. Looking back, I really like Colin's Doctor as he added more depth to the character. We'd had a lot of kind Doctors and I guess it needed balancing out.

Then came McCoy. He was cool and I wished that I was Ace. But then the press reported that there were to be no more series and then they didn't even show all the episodes that were in the 'final' series. I hated the BBC at that time and I was very angry, but I never forgot the Doctor and I used to wish they would bring it back. And then they did.

In 2005 my own life was in crisis. I was at a real low. I had lost a partner and a child, had a brush with cancer and one of my other children was diagnosed autistic. I was hanging on by a thread. And then he came back.

One day I was in the kitchen cooking tea when I heard music. Doctor Who music. I rushed through to the living room to see a trailer. *"Doctor Who.*

Coming soon to BBC One." I couldn't help but feel a little like my Doctor had come so save me in my hour of need. I burst into a huge smile and told my boys about how I had watched Doctor Who when I was a little girl. We counted down the days until the series started and my 4 year old watched as I had when I was that age, glued to the screen. Christopher Eccleston was fantastic and my son's first Doctor. My son, like I had been before him, was upset when his first Doctor died. We soon came to love Tennant's Doctor too. While I thought he was just a little bit sexy, my boy thought he "was brilliant" and we cried together when Rose left. When he regenerated we watched sadly. We didn't want him to go either.

We grew to love Matt together and would try and guess what would happen next and then eagerly await the next instalment to find out. We marvelled at the Pandorica and loved the genius of *The Impossible Astronaut*.

We look forward to the next 50 years of Doctor Who and I hope to be around for the the 100th anniversary, when I will be 89, with my children and their children. I wonder who *their* first Doctor will be!

The Greatest Nightmare in the Galaxy

By Blaine Coughlan, 38. Chelmsford, Essex

One of the very earliest memories I have of my life concerns a nightmare. I can vividly recall the scenario. I'm about four years old and wandering aimlessly through a hot airless desert. The sun is pounding down mercilessly on me and the only respite I discover is a looming metal dome sunken into the vast dusty landscape. Now I'm inside that structure and find myself hopelessly lost within a maze of shiny black walls. Ethereal echoes - part distant technology, part muttering ghosts - sound all around as I venture deeper and deeper into the labyrinthine gloom. It gradually begins to dawn on me that I'm never going to get out. I will be trapped in these disorientating whispering corridors for the rest of my life. Not only that, but something feels wrong. I know instinctively that I'm not safe. The first I know is a tangible sense of creeping dread. The hairs on the back of my neck unpleasantly stir as I hear a faint breathy rumble churning closer and closer...

I'm not alone in here. Something's coming to get me. A sickly burst of adrenaline surges right through me but I don't know which way to run. The rumbling intensifies, becoming louder and larger, seeming to surround me on all sides. Facing only yawning dark walls and turnings whichever way I look, reflecting back my petrified expression like a hall of black mirrors, there's no way of knowing where my approaching tormentor will imminently appear. The only certainty is that it will arrive any second and nothing will be able to stop it. The rising rumble reaches a bone-shaking crescendo as I notice the edge of a malevolent shadow gliding into view. I'm rooted to the spot and it feels like I'm shackled underwater. I can't move and I can't get away and all I can hear is a single word electronically screamed all around me. *"EXTERMINATE!"*

That's when I woke up in a cold sweat and shrieking out for my parents. Considering that the imagery of my dream featured various disparate elements of the 1979 Tom Baker story *Destiny of the Daleks*, there's no doubt that I must have recently seen it. I don't remember watching the episodes but I definitely remember the nightmare. Doctor Who always had an extremely tight grip on me from as early as I can remember. It was always something thrilling, exciting and terrifying. I was definitely an avid viewer and couldn't get enough of these scary adventures featuring the wild manic man with the wild manic scarf and wild manic hair. I do have memories of sitting in front of my parents' big TV as stories from Season 18 were first broadcast with images like the Marshmen and the Melkur very clear in my mind. At this time, I knew little further about the programme. The Doctor was played by Tom Baker, there were lots of different monsters and it had a fabulous but unnerving theme tune which ended with a *"Boom"*! I thought it was a really great show and made sure I watched it whenever I could.

Even from very early on, Doctor Who started to shape my life. In 1984 when I was nine, I was due to be having swimming lessons on a certain weekday evenin until I realised that this would clash directly with Doctor Who. What's more, the next scheduled episode was due to be the regeneration from Peter Davison into Colin Baker. There was no way on God's Earth that I was going to miss that. My parents explained that the lessons had already been booked but I expressed my displeasure in such an outrageous display of tantrums that my parents eventually gave in and dutifully re-booked my swimming lessons for an alternate evening. I love them so much. At the time, of course, we did not own a video recorder. That came in 1987 so, amazingly, I was able to record episodes of Doctor Who and watch them back whenever I fancied.

Since "the second coming" of the programme, Cardiff has become a Mecca for me and I've visited the city several times, firstly in 2006 for the *Children in Need* concert at the Millennium Centre and various occasions since. I've visited the many new exhibitions all over the country, often spending hours at a time just wandering around, lost in a world of Slitheens, Clockwork Robots, Sontarans, Racnos Empresses and Silents. It's difficult to describe the incredible feeling of serenity and contentment I get just being surrounded and enveloped by everything Doctor Who, which is why I've tried to attend every possible live event including the *Doctor Who Proms* at the Royal Albert Hall, *Doctor Who Live* and *The Crash of the Elysium*. The most momentous moment of all came in early 2012 when I returned to Cardiff for the official BBC convention where I was finally able to set foot inside the actual TARDIS during a thrilling set tour to the Roath Lock studios. One of the ladies showing people around the set noted that I didn't stop grinning from the second I stepped through the police box doors. Well, of course I didn't. Doctor Who is my religion and being able to walk up the ramps and down the steps as well as activating several controls on the real-life console on the actual set of the programme is like visiting my own personal Holy Land.

Therefore, over the years, Doctor Who has had the most enormous impact on my life and continues to do so. I literally book time off work every single year to ensure that I never miss the original broadcast of a single new episode. I don't see that situation ever changing and, as the 50th anniversary approaches, with the promise of new episodes, new companions and one of the biggest events in the history of BBC One, I know that my love of Doctor Who is just going to grow and grow and grow. Although one of the very earliest memories I have of my life concerns a nightmare, it was one of the most suspenseful, thrilling and magical nightmares ever, relating to something that has subsequently filled my dreams, and indeed my life, to a utterly galactic level, and I wouldn't have it any other way.

Here's to the next fifty years and I hope I get to experience them all.

The Power of Who

By Paul Hardwick, aged 34, from Australia

Is it the journey? Or the destination? With the Doctor and I, it has been the journey. Memories of my childhood always seem to involve the Doctor and his TARDIS. You could say that they are symbols scattered across my own timeline. It has had a profound impact on my psyche. Never can I recall a time in my life when Doctor Who was not woven in. Earliest memories of my childhood seem to revolve around play time, building my own TARDIS console from a washing basket, or a Dalek from a black swivel chair.

Video recording equipment was not a luxury in my early years. Instead, we had an old tape recording unit. TDK audio tapes. That is how I would recall the episodes. Carefully balancing the microphone against the television, adjusting the volume and simultaneously pressing 'PLAY' and 'RECORD'. Tom Baker's full, rich voice, piping through the TV and laying down onto the tape. I watched the early Tom Baker stories with fascination, not wanting to be dragged away for dinner time. *"Just a few more minutes, Mum!"* I would shout. Afterward, sitting in my bedroom, I would play back the audio tape listening to it as I built Lego Daleks to conquer the not so violent Duplo animals.

As I grew and attended primary school, I could bring Doctor Who into my school work. Grade 4 - Self drawn Cybermen comic books, Grade 5 - paper mache TARDIS, Grade 6 - Doctor Who board game. One particular endeavor was to build an over sized hyperspace transmitter from *The Stones of Blood*. I even managed to rope in a few friends to build it from cardboard tubes and the art room supplies. It took many Dalek "rels" to construct. At least, that is how it seemed.

One by one my bookshelf began filling with Doctor Who books given to me by my parents. Time flew by in high school until I graduated. Next to my photo in our Year 12 year book I wrote the caption *'Reverse the Polarity of the Neutron Flow'*, a homage to show that had carried me through life so far. Later, a couple of trips to England gave me the opportunity to visit *The Who Shop*. It was like paradise, holding every Who related object I could imagine. My treasured item was the Hand Lathed Sonic Screwdriver - heavy and solid, a prize in my collection.

So the years went by and I moved to the USA. While my interest never parted, it wasn't a focus - until, that is, 2004, with the announcement of a new series coming the following year! I eagerly waited for it to return, and when it did, I was pulled straight back in and it became my escape.

My life changed when I met woman who was to become my wife. While she had not yet become influenced by the Doctor, he would slowly wind his way into our family. My wife is very tolerant. Our wedding day was one of compromise. We had agreed that a Dalek and a TARDIS could be sit on our wedding cake and all the cuff links were reduced scaled police boxes, discreetly hidden....

The joy that I had as a child, and admittedly as an adult, is reflected now in my own children. Our time together on a Saturday night has brought us together as a family. Initially they humoured me by watching a few episodes. Little did they know it would start entertaining them to. I now hear the sounds of *"Exterminate! Exterminate!"* in the hallway coming from my son. My daughters often ask to play Doctor Who *Monopoly* and it all fills me with pride knowing that I can enrich their imaginations, just the same as mine was. My children have even begun challenging me with Doctor Who trivia. Classic is my forte, however I am happily put in my place when it comes to the New Series'.

My life between fantasy and reality has become intertwined. It is an obsession, but one at which I gladly accept. You see, the power of Who is that it has such a detailed mythology that it shapes one's mind. From the writers that create the worlds to the visual effects and the actors portraying the characters, I feel privileged to have allowed the show to have had such an impact on who I am today. It makes me very excited to follow the show in minute detail. I'm forever clicking on news sites to gobble up the latest tidbit of rumours. It makes me genuinely happy.

The Doctor and I will continue to travel... and I can't wait!

Becoming a Whovian

By Chris Jones, aged 54, from the US

I first became aware of Doctor Who in the 70's living in upstate New York, USA, when my father would have it on. I recall the Fourth Doctor on our TV quite a bit. While not a big fan then, I have distinctive memories. I had mostly lost interest in Doctor Who until about 2010, when some British friends who were big fans captured my interest. They kept telling I 'have to' watch the show. I started watching in the middle of Series 5 and thought Matt was quite good. I was told I HAD to see David Tennant and that if I did that, I had to see the Ninth Doctor as well to have a complete story. I started over with Series 1, at the time still following the Series 5 on live TV to the end.

Chris was good, it's really too bad he didn't do one more season. Saying that, I have to say that David Tennant brought so much energy and passion to the character. He was so popular that he became seemingly irreplaceable. Matt is great, but my passion for the Doctor lies with David, who made me a true Doctor Who fan.

Space-Age Gloss and My Favourite Hat

By Jacob Edwards, aged 36, from Australia

Pshtooow. Starburst. Not quite four years old, I was eating ice cream - vanilla, square cone - when Doctor Who returned to ABC TV under the auspices of new producer John Nathan-Turner. There were marshmen, vampires, a surreal white nowhere, an evil statue, the Watcher, regeneration...

Season 18, if unlikely to send anyone scurrying behind the sofas of lore, was atmospheric, moody and bewildering and took hold of my formative psyche even while much of the nuance went soaring over my head. Therein followed three seasons of Peter Davison then regeneration again - an explosion of colour and ideas as science fiction cast its spell.

I remember being violently ill one afternoon - food poisoned at lunch by a rhyming slang restaurant chicken, the infamous 'Clara Cluck' - but taking anticipatory comfort on my deathbed and recovering sufficiently to watch episode one of *Vengeance on Varos.* By this stage I'd discovered the Target novelisations (lured, no doubt, by their beautiful if somewhat beguiling covers) and within them the former Doctors I'd glimpsed but fleetingly in the 20th anniversary special. Thus, when Colin Baker disappeared so mysteriously from his 6:30pm time slot, I secured advances on my pocket money, set my sights on collecting every book I could find, and launched myself into the ever-expanding universe of a fully-fledged fan.

The ABC supported this metamorphosis by screening repeats of Patrick Troughton's *The Mind Robber* and *The Krotons*, followed by all of the Jon Pertwee stories. Autons, Axons and Ogrons, Silurians and Sea Devils, Bessie and Benton, UNIT and the Master, Peladon, Ice Warriors, giant maggots and giant spiders, Daemons and Daleks... Pertwee-ere Doctor Who promoted a dialectic, if morally unambiguous, spirit of inquiry, and by the time that Tom Baker came along with his hat and scarf, I found myself suitably prepared for the darker explorations upon which Philip Hinchcliffe and Robert Holmes embarked, skipping blithely through gothic forests and cherry-picking from science fiction's rich, dystopian history...

If my enduring fondness for Doctor Who can be attributed to one aspect in particular, it is that the programme was eye-opening, always. Its action and suspense was tempered by humour and a ceaseless questioning of my young mind. New episodes were proving more and more elusive, and as Colin Baker was discarded and Sylvester McCoy played out his own fleeting tenure, my heightened anticipation of each shortened season slowly gave way to an impending sense of loss. The world was changing. Doctor Who was no longer ubiquitous. My childhood ambition had always been to write. Not necessarily for Doctor Who, although that remains a pipe dream, but as primary school segued to high school and then university, the TARDIS dematerialised from my life and took with it, perhaps, some of that inspiration.

I am a writer these days, my commitment to the craft coinciding, more or less, with Christopher Eccleston's taking up of the Doctor Who mantle in 2005. I am married to a wonderfully Doctor Who tolerant non-Whovian. My son recently declared Sylvester McCoy to be the most awesome Doctor ever (*"Way better than whatshisname, Matt Smith..."*), and while my adult brain might reflexively raise an eyebrow or two at this, childhood's imprint is easily strong enough to have me arguing a case for each of the first seven Doctors. There is, I shall always maintain, good reason to call it 'classic' and not just 'old series' Doctor Who...

Why I Should Be The Next Doctor

By Patrick Magee, aged 26, from Sydney, Australia

Legend has it that my mother watched the show while she was pregnant with me, and the cathode rays emanating from the television induced some kind of nerdy mutation in her unborn child. My earliest memory is of the Dalek shuttle shattering the windows of Coal Hill School, at the end of part three of *Remembrance of the Daleks*. Unlike UK fans - who can accurately pinpoint each childhood memory based on the series' original transmission dates - I have no way of telling exactly when this was, but it must have been around 1989 or so.

It's probably a disappointment to my family that, rather than remembering my first glimpse of snow, or the birth of my baby sister, what mattered most to young Patrick Magee was a pretty sweet spaceship smashing up a beacon of government-funded education.

As a child, my most treasured possession was a battered copy of the 1983 Radio Times special, held together with sticky tape and Eric Saward's turgid prose. It was from the pages of that hallowed tome that I first learnt about the five actors who had played the various incarnations of television's greatest hero, and it was then that my innocent mind set an irrevocable and financially untenable destiny: I was going to become an actor, so that one day I could be the Doctor.

Of course, I was slightly hampered by the fact that I grew up in the Wilderness Years - that dark, lonely period between 1989 and 2005 when, like a shoal of desperate and socially inept sharks, we eagerly swallowed whatever half-baked chum with a logo on it that was thrown at us from the back of the BBC Worldwide boat.

No matter, thought the child version of me, I'll while away the hours until the show comes back by writing my own novel, a story too broad and deep for the small screen that those stuffed shirts at the BBC would never have the guts to show on television...

When I was fourteen (some four years after I'd burst into tears at the end of the TV Movie, crying that "it wasn't Doctor Who" while my stoic Northern Irish grandparents looked on embarrassedly) it dawned on me that I wouldn't stand any chance of playing the Doctor with my Australian accent. So I did what any reasonable teenager would do in that situation: every night in my sleep, I listened to the *Talkin 'Bout My Regeneration* CD that came free with Doctor Who Magazine #279 to celebrate the launch of Big Finish's audio Doctor Who range. And over the course of a year, my voice slowly evolved into the

Was I bullied about it at school? Hell yes I was. But every taunt and jibe and snipe was worth it, because that stupid accent was one step closer to becoming the Doctor.

In 2005, the show finally returned to the air. In a weird turn of events, the BBC misspelt my name as "Christopher Eccleston" on all the publicity material and then followed it up by completely forgetting to cast me, a decision they're probably still ruing to this day. But Doctor Who was back, and, more importantly, it was fantastic.

Twenty-some years after my first fateful decision, I was an actor. By most accounts, I'm pretty good at it. Being a pretty good actor, of course, is not quite enough to make a living in this country, but that's the risk you run by living in the sun-drenched and home-renovation-reality-TV-obsessed paradise that is Australia. So I did what any reasonable young man would do: I abandoned all my friends and burgeoning career in the exciting field of car-dealership related advertising and I moved to London. There, I took a method-acting class on the basis that Louise Jameson (Leela) would be running it and Richard Franklin (Mike Yates) hired me to proof-read his novel! In March, I played a frog footman in a very silly, very wonderful Cinderella play written by the filthily talented Arthur Darvill, and we all got very tipsy afterwards...

At the Edinburgh Fringe, where I was performing my solo stand-up show, I met the wonderful Toby Hadoke and John Dorney, both of them fine writers and performers and actively involved in the world of Doctor Who. They were two incredibly inspiring men who were making a living from being Doctor Who fans. Before I left Australia, I had no idea such a thing could exist. It belonged firmly in the realms of fantasy, like dragons or Daleks or decent policy from David Cameron. I followed the two of them around Edinburgh like a lovelorn puppy, until they finally caved in to my affection, and now I'm proud to call myself their casual acquaintance.

After the Fringe, I was homeless for a period of close to two months, because of a broken heart and the fact that my primitive amphibian brain cannot make plans further than two days in advance. Now, I should stress that it wasn't a completely dire situation. I had a good network of wonderful friends who generously offered couches and beds and blow-up mattresses to crash on. But London in the autumn is not an ideal place to be sleeping rough. I spent one night under Southwark Bridge and another in a shop doorway in Camden Town with only a stray cat and some salami for warmth.

It was then that I decided it was time to come home.

So here I am, back in Australia, still trying to carve a living for myself in this cut-throat industry. Life is, on the whole, good, even if it's becoming increasingly clear that I'm never going to play the Doctor. But that's okay. Life's like that. You get over it. And then the news came through, along with a series of increasingly tenuous puns revolving around the words "who" and "time" - Matt Smith is leaving Doctor Who.

Which means there's an opening. A tiny crack in the fabric of the universe that (for example) a twenty-something actor with an inexplicable British accent could crawl inside and find himself at the helm of the TARDIS, in that mysterious place where time and space are one (Wales).

Hartnell. Troughton. Pertwee. Baker. Davison. Baker. McCoy. McGann. Eccleston. Tennant. Smith... Magee?

Meeting by Chance

A poem by Veronika Kuncová, aged 20, from Czech Republic

Waistcoat and appearance of gentleman,
Soul of romantic and curly hair,
He has two hearts and he is a half human.
This kind of being is really rare.

Surely you know who I mean?
Who was my first of all Time Lords,
Who travels in a blue time machine,
And knows every violin chord.

Now there is absolutely no doubt
That he is totally great,
That I am talking about
Incarnation number eight.

When I saw the movie for the first time
I couldn't believe my eyes,
And now I can not find a good rhyme.
But it was a big surprise.

One night I had a dream.
I remember it clearly,
Street hidden in the steam.
And I was walking quickly.

Suddenly I heard a noise behind my back,
It was that weird blue box.
And a quiet whisper sounding like that:
"My life goes by tick tock."

"Come with me!" I followed him and went inside.
I could hardly stand.
"Wait a minute, it's smaller on the outside!"
And he just took my hand.

Time And Relative Dimension In Space,
She is huge, as you can see.
I've noticed worry in your face,
"So, what about a cup of tea?"

Purely and simply:
Eight is my favourite
And that is true.
My favourite Doctor.

Me and Who

By Martin Backman, aged 27, from Finland

My first experience with Doctor Who was the when 1996 TV movie with Paul McGann aired on Finnish television during Easter 1999. Admittedly, it was a very confusing introduction to the franchise, as there was constantly a sense of missing out on something. It also didn't help that the protagonist was almost immediately killed off and replaced by another man!

After that I was vaguely aware of Doctor Who, among other things, seeing it listed on the *Guinness Book of Records*. So when Series 1 aired on Finnish TV during my military service, I caught a glimpse of a few random scenes here and there. During a study trip to Dublin, I entered a Forbidden Planet store where I saw a room full of Doctor Who toys and other merchandise. I was aware of its existence, but it wasn't until November 2009, ten years after I had seen McGann's outing, that I sat down and watched a story in its entirety.

The Waters of Mars had just aired and a Whovian friend wanted to show it to me to get me hooked. Well, it certainly worked and I proceeded to track down Series 1 through to 4 and managed to watch them all before *The End of Time* premiered.

When I had watched the bulk of the Russell T Davies era, there were still a few weeks left until *The End of Time*, so I proceeded to watch several episodes from the Classic Series too. Now that I have been a fan for a little over three years, I've developed my opinions of the franchise. My two favourite periods of the show are the Russell T Davies era and most of 1970s Doctor Who, both of which I find to be very similar in fun and adventurous content. While I like all Doctors in different ways, I have four Doctors in particular that I especially enjoy. These are Christopher Eccleston, Tom Baker and David Tennant, whom I like equally, but my number one favourite Doctor is Jon Pertwee. Pertwee's Doctor is impossibly cool, a charming gentleman adventurer and gadget-wielding super spy who would put even James Bond to shame. Because I enjoy Pertwee's action filled adventures so much, I sincerely hope that there will again be a Doctor like him, preferably played by a tough-looking middle aged actor who'll drive around on wild chases with Bessie...

Fragments of Impossible Worlds

By KRING D., aged 24, from the Philippines

My mind has a sickness. Each waking day, I cannot find the reason to appreciate reality as it is. I always find a way to believe that, somewhere, a deep puddle may be the door to an unknown universe where mud-folk lived. A car abandoned in a field in the middle of nowhere hides a secret room from another dimension, and that, beyond the glass in my mirror, is reality. My daydreams are fragments of my otherworldly memories. Among these daydreams, I met the Doctor.

I was already having adventures before I actually met him, and that only increased our chances of bumping onto each other. I was once a hitchhiker, travelling through space and eventually knowing the answer to the ultimate question of the universe. That's when I heard about the Doctor.

I gradually grew out of my little world and sadly made myself a mechanical slave of the corporate world. My mind was dying. My spirit gone. And none was left to revive the faith I used to have in my dreams. My sickness shrivelled to a bitterly realistic illness called 'depression'.

I isolated myself from other people. Discourses with them became dull and dead. I found myself seemingly speaking another language, a language incoherent to these human creatures. A language that for all I knew could have been dead for years, only to be revived by my own introspective isolation. I lost belief in myself and everything I did, ultimately losing all purpose.

Then I met some strange friends. I found them bathing themselves in prose, poetry and beer on top a mountain one night, most beautifully speaking the same language that I thought I alone would understand. I found a welcoming embrace from this strange group of people. And through them, I finally met the Doctor.

With his many faces, I love the Doctor's wide-eyed, child-like fascination for all things new and old. Never cynical, always open to welcome a new species, race or idea.

The Doctor reawakened everything that I thought I had forgotten. He gave me back my mind and all that I had lost faith in. After seeing his adventures, I thought the world was beautiful again and I was brave enough to step onto puddles or celebrate my existence from the other side of the mirror, rediscovering that secret world that I always knew existed. And that through any experience, the human mind can transcend beyond cruelty, illness or death. As he did to Vincent, a man I knew very well through his sickness, the Doctor made me see again that I am never alone or insignificant. In the vast and wide expanse of multiple realities, each and every existence is never without purpose. I am a golden piece of movement that partakes in the becoming of things. My existence as a being makes certain things true that should be true and will never be true should I not exist. And because of this realisation, I found my mind again. I then finally revived a strong belief in one single truth that I, as a child and as an adult, I always and always should believe in. I am.

My mind has a sickness. Each waking day, is a marvellous reality of colour and wonder. I have been to the world underneath the puddles, in a box concealing another dimension, and to the time beyond the mirror and the fireplace. My dreams are fragments of memories of impossible, incredible and unbelievable worlds.

Among these dreams, I travel with the Doctor.

Getting to Know the Doctor

By JC2006, aged 26, from the UK

I grew up during an era when there was no Doctor Who. I was born not long before they decided to cancel the show and since the 1996 TV movie wasn't that well known and none of my family watched the show, I wasn't really interested. I knew of terms such as Dalek and TARDIS, everyone did, but other than that, I really only considered it an old sci-fi show that used to be popular years before I was born with special effects very much of its era, men in costumes and wobbly sets.

Subsequently, when Russell T Davies worked with his team to bring Doctor Who back, I didn't immediately start watching. I had a lot of things going on in my life and TV didn't mean all that much to me, so I actually missed the first new series in 2005. Since I hadn't been interested in Doctor Who before, I didn't see why I would be now.

That all changed in December 2005. I don't remember the exact circumstances, but what I do remember clearly was seeing the moment Christopher Eccleston regenerated. I vaguely knew different actors had played the Doctor, but I'm not sure I knew much about regeneration. So I watched as the Ninth Doctor said goodbye to Rose and energy exploded from his body with special effects that certainly weren't available in the 60s and 70s. The sight and sound of it was like nothing I'd seen before, as one Doctor was replaced by another, picking up the conversation as if nothing had happened. *Barcelona, not the city, the planet, where dogs have no noses...*

From that moment, I started watching Doctor Who. As a creative person who enjoys writing, I loved the ideas that filled the show. The Doctor, a 900 year old Time Lord that could regenerate to avoid death. The spectacle of the TARDIS materialising and dematerialising to the distinctive sound of those engines and learning that far from just being a mechanical time machine that just happened to look like a police pox, it was a living machine. I loved the idea of the Time War, an ultimate battle between the Time Lords and the Daleks from which the Doctor was the only survivor.

This all served to draw me into the show. It was high quality sci-fi, it was brand new but had stacks and stacks of back story that gave it substance in a way it could never have had if they'd rebooted the show.

My enjoyment of the show only increased with Doctor Who Confidential. We were introduced to the man that had brought Doctor Who back and made the revival possible, Russell T Davies, and I saw in him a man that loved and was enthusiastic about the show. Writing it was clearly his dream come true and that was quite something, considering how the reality of making the show could have crushed that. With Julie Gardner and Phil Collinson, you had a team that seemed to get on really well together and loved the show as much as Russell did.

I've been unwell for most of my adult life and there has always been good reason for me to feel deep negativity. When the Tenth Doctor literally burst on to my screen, I found a source of escapism that I hadn't experienced in many years. Here was a man that smiled all the time. He was energetic, enthusiastic and was full of wonder about life and the universe. That was positive in a way I can never experience, and yet he possessed a hidden negativity that I could identify and empathise with. For those reasons, for getting me into Doctor Who and for providing me with escapism and positivity I can never find myself, David Tennant as the Tenth Doctor was my Doctor and remains so to this day.

In closing, there is one other thing I'd like to speak about, and that's the Doctor Who fan community of WhovianNet. At the time of writing, I've posted 932 comments on the site, making me the third highest poster ever. What I've always liked about WhovianNet is that everyone knows each other. It's a place where classic and revived fans with their own favourite Doctors meet and talk to each other after every episode and important news story. It's true we don't always agree, but I've been impressed by how our community manages to stay civil and respectful, largely agreeing to disagree when we do.

I hope the BBC remembers that the show lives symbiotically with its fans and what they think really *does* matter.

An Unearthly Delivery

By Dakota Lopez, aged 21, from New York, USA

I didn't grow up on Doctor Who. I didn't even catch the first episode of Eccleston's run on air. Or Tennant. Or Smith. I didn't begin watching until Series 6 had finished airing. So how did I get involved? I was bored, really. My favourite show growing up, *Smallville*, had just finished it's impressive 10 year run and I needed something new to fill the void. Badly. So, naturally, I typed "longest science fiction series of all time" into Google, understandably expecting *Star Trek* to pop up. But it didn't. Instead, this funny little British programme called Doctor Who showed up. I had heard about it before, seen it on shirts and such, but I needed to know more. After all my research, after all the preparation, nothing really prepared me for all the wonders and love and heartbreak that the show would inspire within me.

I used my personal *Netflix* account and chose to begin where most today do - at the beginning of the 2005 reboot series. I didn't instantly fall in love, no, but the fact that each story was so different, in both theme and genre, was proof alone to me of the endless possibilities a show of this type could inspire. What a gem I had found!

And then it happened. My dreams were crushed. The first season had passed and so too had the Ninth Doctor's era. This crushing was short-lived as I witnessed my first regeneration. And it was *"fantastic"*.

I've tried to watch the Classic series from *An Unearthly Child* onwards, but the reconstructions were particularly difficult to get past. So I just started buying some of the DVDs here and there. I started with *The Robots of Death* and since then I haven't been able to get enough. I now have over 50 Classic stories on DVD. I even got my copy of *Earthshock* signed by Peter Davison at New York Comic Con, to which I wore my custom Tennant suit!

You're still probably wondering why I titled this 'An Unearthly Delivery'. Well, I happen to be one of the Americans who got their copy of the Series 7: Part 2 Blu-ray a week before the season had even ended. I pre-ordered the item about 2 months prior to receiving it, and honestly forgot about it until it had arrived. Learning the truth about Clara before 99.99% of the world was quite something. But let me tell you, when John Hurt popped up onto my screen at the end I nearly screamed - I definitely jumped off the couch at the very least. I had a secret on my hands that was far too great for me to hold onto. Possibly one of the biggest reveals in all of Who history...

I posted pictures onto my Instagram feed and the next day I posted a few onto Tumblr. *That's* when things got crazy. I went from about 17 followers to nearly 400 in one day. Over 2,000 reblogs later and the media got hold of my pictures. Perhaps it was infantile that I posted pictures online. Many thought that I was just bragging, but that really wasn't my intention. I was emailed by BBC America and even phoned shortly afterwards asking that I don't reveal any spoilers or put the episode online. I obliged their request.

I am proud to be a fan of Doctor Who. There is no other show with such longevity. There's no other show that adapts with the times so seamlessly. Truly there is no other show like it. It may not be the best produced or have the greatest track record of good episodes, and it definitely doesn't have the greatest track record when it comes to getting full seasons out on a yearly basis, but it's *my* show. And it always will be.

Turn Right

By Tom Buxton, aged 19, from the UK

"I can see... a man. The most remarkable man. How did you meet him?"

"You're supposed to tell me."

"You turned right. But what if you turned left? What then?"

It's Saturday 18th June 2005. I'm casually tucking into dinner at a friend's abode and it occurs to me that there's a television set switched onto BBC One to my right. A dilemma confronts me, as two scenarios come to mind. I can turn left, simply ignoring whatever's being broadcast in favour of what's remaining on my plate, or alternatively I can turn right, and witness the programme that's about to air on that alluring screen in a few seconds' time...

In a split second, under the environmental conditioning of factors which can only be called chance and random circumstance, my gaze switches to the screen, and my discovery of Doctor Who begins. Sure, I had heard murmurings of this mysterious science fiction cult drama ever since its return earlier that year. Aside from the odd glance on Saturday evenings as genius episodes like *Rose, Dalek* and *Father's Day* were broadcast on a weekly basis, though, I had come into no form of direct contact with Doctor Who until that fortuitous evening

45 minutes later and my whole world had changed. My 10 year old self came to realise the kind of wonder and awe a brave drama such as this could inspire in a young, impressionable viewer such as myself. As *The Parting of the Ways* drew to a climax, and as one man stepped into his time machine, burdened by the weight of his travels, only to change his entire face and personality in an explosion of yellow energy, one thing became as clear as a Metebilis III crystal. I would never stop watching this show.

Fast forward to Monday 18th June 2007 and that mantra hadn't changed. Quite the opposite, in fact. Having perused *WHSmith's* DVD aisles ever since that fateful dinner, I'd picked up a great number of Classic stories from Doctor Who's past, including *Genesis of the Daleks, The Caves of Androzani* and *The Time Warrior*. Using these enlightening materials as foundations, my 12 year old self was now a more confident viewer of Doctor Who, his subscription to Doctor Who Magazine secured and knowledge of his favourite show's history now well established by DVDs, reference books and an increasingly useful online domain known as *Wikipedia*.

They say that the more things change, the more they stay the same. In the case of that particular Monday morning, no cliché could have rang more true than that one. Stepping back onto my secondary school minibus in the closing days of Year 7, two directional scenarios lay before me. I could turn left, popping the iPod on and ignoring a wealth of thrilling conversations with one of my closest friends on the hottest topic of them all, or I could turn right and do the complete opposite. Given the raw excitement *Utopia* had filled me with just two days before, just as *Parting* had two years before that, the choice here was obvious. I joined my mate and brilliant discussions regarding who this 'Master' character was and his implications within the upcoming two-part finale were ensued...

What with this growing list of positive sentiments and anecdotes, it would perhaps seem only apt for me to now recall another such moment of pride found in being a fan of Doctor Who. As I write this piece on Wednesday 24th July 2013, though, that does not seem to be entirely the case on the surface. By the time you read this, I have no doubt that the Comic Con 50th anniversary special trailer fiasco will be well and truly out of your mind, but right now, I'm seeing Twitter ablaze with angry commenters who are furious that another audience in another nation has been allowed a glimpse at the episode before we have here in the UK.

Given that I know and accept the exclusivity of Comic Con's offerings, two scenarios once again arise. Do I turn left, away from the shame of a fan base which on rare occasions produces such a rowdy minority? The answer remains clear, however. Even now, I still will always turn right. In this case, it's a computer screen I turn to face, as I discuss my feelings on the worldwide status of Doctor Who with other avid followers of the show in this time of heated discussion, and realise once again the strength of not only my own passion for this now legendary programme, but indeed the strength of passions the world over.

In truth, it is this unyielding, universal and indeed seemingly eternal passion for the show that will always force this particular viewer to turn right. When I use the word 'right', of course, there are multiple connotations of the term, and by this point, as a 19 year old viewer who still remains inspired by the travels of a 1,000 year old alien, I can confirm that 'right' can now be placed in a context of morals rather than direction. No matter what minor ill tidings may occasionally arise around advance screenings, anniversaries or the Abzorbaloff, Doctor Who will always remain nothing less than the right choice of viewing for millions of kids and adults alike across the planet, regardless of age or social demographic.

Even those elements of the show which do inspire a heated reaction can often be turned to the advantage of a fan such as myself, in terms of summarising our feelings for Doctor Who and our role within its seemingly immortal legacy. In this case, I'll use the words of *Love and Monster*'s Elton Pope as a foundation on which to base my closing sentiments...

"You know when you're a kid, they tell you it's all 'Grow up, get a job, get married, have a kid'? Nah. There's more to life than that. There's the

chance, on top of all that, to find yourself whisked away from ordinary life to new worlds with new stories. Sometimes, the truth is that Doctor Who is so much stranger than our ordinary lives. Sometimes, it's so much darker and so much madder. But keep it with you through the years, carry its legacy with you throughout all of your experiences, because one thing is for sure. Life is so much better for it."

Fighting Daleks

By Melda Uytun, aged 23, from Turkey

I am a full time believer. And unfortunately I am disappointed to see that the universe holds many secrets and adventures that it never shows. Maybe that's only because I am not among the "chosen" people.

If I write about welcoming Doctor Who into my miserably dull life, I have to mention my willingness about having sci-fi adventures, or magically finding myself in Middle Earth or Hogwarts. This passion separates myself from other people who are pleased to have normal lives. So, Doctor Who was just another stop for me, but at the same time, one of the greatest stories that will stay with me for as long as I live.

When I first started watching the series with the Ninth Doctor and Rose, they took me to another dimension. Even the silliest kind of villains were terrifying for me because the writers of Doctor Who are the masters of creating stories that include horror, thrills, science fiction, friendship and love. Basically, they are the master of everything. Every episode is deep. Every companion is real.

With Rose I fell in love with the Doctor, it wasn't important if she was Nine or Ten, I loved both. With Rose I was stuck in a parallel universe and I wasn't satisfied with Rose's new life with a copy of Ten, and I cried. I cried too much. If crying over fictional characters at this age is stupid, then I don't care about being stupid.

With Martha I experienced the end of the world, I saw that family is the most important thing when it comes to be a human being. I became a tough and determined woman and walked the Earth. I knew that Martha was desperately in love with Ten but he was in love with somebody else. This is something almost every one of us goes through. I felt Martha's despair and when she decided to quit time travelling, I wasn't upset for her. For the first time I thought it was a proper ending.

With Donna I discovered the dynamics of having a friendship with the Doctor. I visited one of my favourite authors, Agatha Christie, and I became very fond of Donna's sense of humour. She was a living example of the best friend that everybody should have, but when it came to the time when we had to say goodbye to Donna, I was angry, very angry, that everything fell apart and Donna had to forget everything she had lived with Ten. I can't forget Donna, because Donna was my friend.

With Amy and Rory, I realised that there may be ups and downs in every relationship but what really matters is that you should never lose the connection that you made when you first met that beautiful, great person. Amy and Rory always had to end up together, and they did. They were two different people but their stories weren't separate from each other. They were one together.

The deeper I fell into the Whoniverse, the more I started to realise some feelings growing in me. I was becoming a believer of the Doctor. I *believed* in the Doctor's existence. And I couldn't escape because it felt so right, he was real - maybe in another dimension, or in another universe, but he's out there. I can't just say it's just a show, because it isn't. It's in my life. Wherever I go, if I see and accidentally look at a statue, I get frightened and flee.

I have to believe that all of these things actually had happened and that more will happen. The Doctor is alive. Personally, I'd like to fight Daleks instead of fighting life. Life is dull. Daleks are not. They would at least exterminate the dullness of life!

Talkin' 'Bout My Regeneration
By Marcus Cooke, aged 36, from the UK

My adventure with the Doctor began in March 2005. But first, I have a confession. I was never much of a Doctor Who fan. Being a comic book and sci-fi nerd, I was well aware of who and what the Doctor was and what the show was about. I visited Longleat Safari Park's Doctor Who Exhibition when I was a wee boy and remember quite vividly the Sylvester McCoy episode with the Candy Man, so I was already pretty familiar with the series.

In 1996, it was Colin Baker himself who told me it was a *"fantastic world to discover"* - or words to that effect. It wasn't until the series came back after a 16 year absence that I would finally become a fan.

But which Doctor would be *my* Doctor? I loved Christopher Eccleston but David Tennant just clinched it for me. The Tenth Doctor displayed a cheeky, playful, easy going side but also had a vengeful and unforgiving streak with a tendency to babble, as opposed to the Ninth Doctor's battle weary and quite intense persona. Both were heroic, but the Tenth Doctor just looked and acted cool, wearing his suit, his long flowing coat and his *amazing* hair. Yet as an alien Time Lord, he displayed a spectrum of human emotions and, though he had companions, you got the sense that he was alone in the universe. To some extent, he was.

My favourite aspect in Doctor Who is the Doctor's biological ability to regenerate when he is close to death. The idea of a character that can change his face and personality becoming a new man was a big draw, while simultaneously replacing the actor when he wishes to retire from the role was nothing short of genius. This in itself makes Doctor Who unique. In 2008, David Tennant announced he was leaving and would "regenerate" at Christmas. I felt devastated. I would watch the Specials leading up to his last episode and in those final moments, something very odd happened to me.

I wept.

You can picture the scene. A 32 year old man crying into his crisp packet, flowing tears the kind Paul Gascoigne would be proud of. I felt like I had lost a friend. The only thing that would keep me going is the fact the Doctor would live on, this time in the form of the magnificent Matt Smith.

I needed more. I went out and - utilising every penny of my hard earned wages - bought the Series 1 to 4 box sets and the Specials. And then it snowballed. Suddenly, the shelf became full of Doctor Who action figures, a

Doctor Who poster materialised in the hallway, and I would scour the Sunday car boot sales hunting old videos and books. I became obsessed.

For me, it's not just the monsters, the acting or the fantastic storytelling. The most special part of watching any Doctor Who episode is sitting with my 5 year old boy, who loves the show, and now he himself has quite a collection of Doctor Who memorabilia. He even built his own TARDIS, aged 3, at pre-school. I would spend hours making up stories about the mad man in the blue box. I see the wonder and curiosity of the Doctor in his eyes, and that's what makes the show so special. It brings generations together and it creates mad conversations down the pub. It's fantastic entertainment for all the family and I cannot wait to see what the next fifty years will bring.

The Bond Across the Ocean

By Allison K. White, aged 16, from the USA

Doctor who? Before *Rose* first aired in the United States, I had no idea of the history and fantastical stories that lived in the world known as Doctor Who. I wish I could recall the exact date that I discovered the existence of it, but it was just a normal day like any other. I remember my Dad coming home from work to our small-town apartment, sitting down in front of the TV, and reading from one of his entertainment magazines. I would usually sit on the couch next to his recliner and watch TV with him, and on that particular day, while watching some random show, he turned to me - a rarely seen smile on his face - to tell me of the return of his all time favourite, childhood TV show. A show called Doctor Who.

In the days before the newest series aired, I remember my Dad telling me about the show and how he used to love watching it and that his favorite Doctor - not going to lie, I thought he meant a medical doctor at first - was a man named Tom Baker. I was thrilled to see him excited and truly happy about something again, especially after the rough separation that he and my Mom had gone through not too long before. Sure, the revival of one of his childhood pleasures was not enough to make him not stressed anymore or his hours of working to support my brother and me turn enjoyable, but I think it gave him something to look forward to, and that was good enough for me.

And I'm glad that I decided to become a part of it all

After watching *Rose*, I was hooked, something that I'm sure made my Dad really happy. Not only was he able to share a part of his childhood with me, but it gave the two of us a set time when we would get together and simply spend time together. I was grateful for the hour long sessions when we would sit and wonder at what else the characters - especially the magical duo of the Doctor and Rose - would have to face next.

And I started to love the show for much more than just the fact that I felt like I could connect to the average-girl character of Rose. My love for it means so much more than just my love for the amazing duo of David Tennant and Billie Piper and for the wonderful essence of mystery that I find in every new episode. From the get-go, I really felt like my eyes were being opened to a new world. And as cheesy as that sounds, it was so *true*.

At that time in my life, I had only left Illinois once and that was when I was six. I'd never left the country or gone to Disneyland. Heck, I never really went anywhere beyond the two counties that my parents lived in. To little ten year old me, Illinois was the world. Well, until Doctor Who came along, that is.

A few episodes in, my Dad became acquainted with a man who lives over in Scotland - Ronnie is his name - and the two instantly bonded over Doctor Who. They still talk about it to this day. I remember being completely surprised at how my Dad was actually talking to someone who lives across the Atlantic Ocean. I'll admit it took me a while to believe him! Anyway, after having a little taste of what existed on the other side of the ocean, I craved more.

My love for Doctor Who led to my love for other British shows, which blossomed into my love for other cultures - the first one being that of Britain. Because of Doctor Who, my respect for other countries and what they have to offer has grown. I learned to love other languages and I began to slowly surround myself with works of entertainment from other parts of the world, especially those of Japan and Britain. And if you were to ask anyone in my family, they could tell you exactly how much influence these other countries have had on my life.

When I think back on it, to the time before I was exposed to Doctor Who, I can't help but wonder what my life would have been like without it. For some reason, I have always had trouble with trying to imagine a land that exists across the oceans and seas. During the younger times in my life, it was just impossible for me. I don't think I was aware of the fact that people in other countries even made movies or TV shows or novels. I may not have even considered the idea of people actually *living* in a place thousands of miles away. My world was small and unknowing. And Doctor Who changed that.

Sharing stories that help people from all over the world connect with each other emotionally and allow them to learn about lifestyles different than their own - *that's* what being a Whovian means to me. Doctor Who is so much more than just a story to enjoy with those around you. It's a chance to discover and join in on a bond that has been forming between people everywhere as they travel on with the wonderfully impossible Doctor in a way that makes them seem like they are *all* his companions. This bond - a bond full of happiness, tears, mysteries, and fears - has lived on for 50 years. And for the sake of all of those who live in a closed off world like I did and are in need of a good story like I was, I hope that it will continue on for many more years to come.

Thank you, Doctor Who.

It Began at the End of the World

By Lucy Boulter, aged 17, from the UK

I entered the world of Doctor Who on Saturday 2nd April 2005, the day *The End Of The World* was first broadcast. I was 8 years old, curled up on the sofa and I remember looking at the TV, not really knowing what I was even watching. The first thing I remember seeing was this small, fat, blue creature, followed by a human tree and a talking piece of stretched skin. Even from watching less than 5 minutes of this unusual but fantastical programme, I knew I loved it. As the episode carried on, I fell in love with it more and more, right up until the end credits, when that spectacular music started playing.

Since then, I have collected merchandise, from the figurines to all of the new DVDs, from Doctor Who Adventures to three remote controlled Daleks, and from storybooks to a 50th anniversary necklace. I just love so many things about Doctor Who - the exciting storylines which also break your heart, the scary monsters which you kind of have to love, and of course that hypnotic theme tune which I run towards whenever I hear it. Even the sound of the TARDIS makes me sit still.

But it's the *characters* who I really love. They've given us excitement, sadness and a small amount of romance. I have to say my favourite companion was Rose. However, Clara Oswald is in a very close second place. In 2006, I was lucky enough to meet and receive autographs from some of the Doctor Who crew. I met Terry Molloy (Davros), Anna Hope (Novice Hame), Paul Marc Davis (Chieftain in *Utopia*), Anneke Wills (Polly Wright) and even Colin Baker (The Sixth Doctor)! Yesterday I bought tickets to the 50th Anniversary Celebration!

After being a Doctor Who fan for more than half of my life, I suppose I look at life a bit differently than I used to. Although I know that Doctor Who is, unfortunately, not real, I sometimes think, "What if there *are* things out there, millions of miles away, right out into space? What if there *is* a man out there, a really mad man... a man who wears tweed and loves bowties?"

Is there really a police box traveling though time and space and twirling around in the vortex? Could there really be, as the stories say... a mad man in a box...?

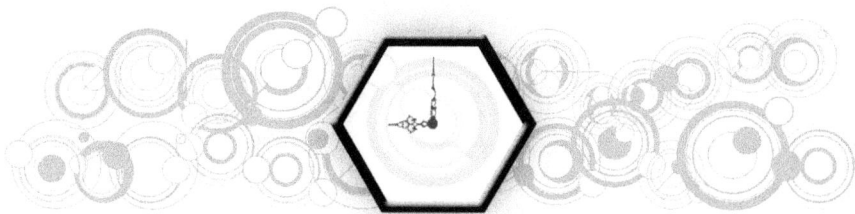

New Zealand, New Who

By Zac Hadley, aged 21, from New Zealand

I have been a Whovian since 2005, when I first started watching Christopher Eccleston as the Ninth Doctor. Before 2005, though, I had little to no knowledge of Doctor Who whatsoever. I had seen or heard mentions of the series, specifically the Classic episodes, as well as glimpses of the Second Doctor, and maybe others, but I never really knew who he was.

When I saw a preview for the return of Doctor Who in 2005 I was curious about it at the time, vaguely remembering having heard of it before. After seeing the first few episodes of Series 1 of the revived series, I thought *"Yeah, I quite like this!"* with a smile.

It might have been, maybe partially, something to do with the episode *The Parting of the Ways*, though exactly what it was that got me into Doctor Who so much I can't really say or explain. The series is unique and completely different from any other. It's a combination of sci-fi, thriller, adventure, mildly supernatural plus all the other genres that define the show. Because of this, it never fails to captivate us fans with its unique stories and characters and villains, and it is even interesting to those who aren't fans and enthusiasts of the show.

Doctor Who has influenced or had an influence on the sort of person I am today in ways I can't quite explain. It has done so in a positive way in terms of my personality and being myself.

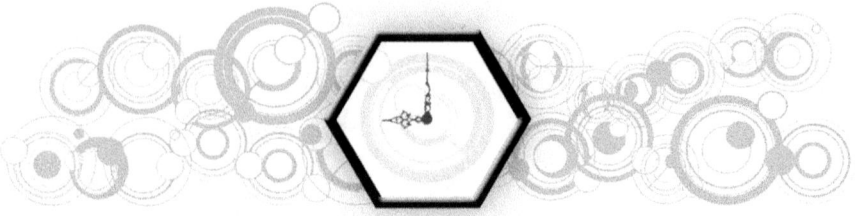

The Show That Conquered
Time and Space

By Richard Coles, aged 18, from the UK

My Doctor Who journey began in 2005 at 10 years old when my Dad sat me down to watch *Rose*. I loved every minute of it and it made such a deep impression on me that 8 years later I'm still a die hard Whovian who lives and breathes the endless well of enjoyment that we call 'the Whoniverse'. I don't go a day without thinking of the show, browsing on WhovianNet or doing *something* related to it. It is my hobby and my lifestyle and I wouldn't have it any other way.

Arguably though, it started before that. Even prior to when I knew about Doctor Who, I was semi-aware of it. I'm a massive fan of *Mr. Bean* and used to watch the episodes endlessly when I was younger, so that means that I must've seen the seen in *Merry Christmas, Mr. Bean* in which he plays around with the toy Dalek in the nativity scene. As to what I thought of it, I can't quite remember. A slightly less hazy memory comes from seeing an advert on TV featuring Richard E. Grant's animated Doctor to promote the BBC Doctor Who website when *Scream of the Shalka* was released. I remember being drawn to it back then and liking what I saw on the advert, even feeling sort of familiar with it. Maybe it's like Arthur Darvill said once, that people seem to be born with a knowledge of Doctor Who, of what a TARDIS is, much in the same way you just seem to know about *Robin Hood, Merlin* or *Sherlock Holmes*. It's either that or reincarnation. Take your pick.

One of the things that strike me about the programme's success is its ability to change the way you look at ordinary, everyday objects and make them sinister. Thanks to this scare-tactic I can never look at shop window dummies or stone statues in the same way ever again. The other thing is its adaptability. This is a show that can be made again and again in the future due to its central concept of infinite possibilities that lay within the TARDIS. It may be possible that one day in the far, far future, fans could be watching The 143 Doctors on their vid-screens using holograms to bring back past Doctors, including the controversial female ones, in a 48 hour special. Then, thousands of years from now, it could take longer than the average life span of a human to watch the entirety of Doctor Who (currently it takes 15 days, 8 hours and 52 minutes to watch up to *The Name of the Doctor*). I love speculating about the future of the show. It's just so fascinating.

In 2008 I picked up my first copy of Doctor Who Magazine, issue 401, which I still get today, and in 2012 I was lucky enough to attend the official Doctor Who Convention where I got to meet my favourite Doctor, Matt Smith, and possibly my favourite companion, Karen Gillan, to get their autographs on a script extract from the end of *The Doctor, the Widow and the Wardrobe* which everyone queuing up was given for them to sign. They also signed my copy of *The Brilliant Book 2012* to add to Nicholas Briggs' autograph which I had picked up earlier. The signed script extract now hangs proudly on my wall, framed for all to see. Steven Moffat also happened to sit directly in front of me and my parents that day, funnily enough. We were sitting in an area of lots of empty fold-out chairs in the foyer of the Millennium Centre, watching a talk from some of the people who help restore old episodes and I'd quickly popped off to the toilet. When I returned, I saw him sitting there in the row in front of my parents and just smiled in amazement as I went to sit back down. Then I just stared at the back of his head, not believing this was actually happening. To top all that, when the Convention was over, there was a free trip to the TARDIS set at Upper Boat Studios. That was fantastically wonderful, fiddling with the Zig-Zag Plotter and seeing the Wibbly Lever. Something I'll never forget.

Even in the TV show there are still things to be discovered when you think you know everything. And so, as I reached *The Five Doctors* - a story I've seen many times before - in my Doctor Who marathon, I found out something new. It was near the end where Sarah Jane says, "It was nice meeting you" to the Fifth Doctor. The Third Doctor replies, "It was nice meeting you too, Sarah Jane," revealing that he had come from a point in his timeline where Sarah Jane wasn't his companion yet. Somehow, this didn't click before and just passed me by, but now that I've noticed it I've realised that it showcases Doctor Who's ultimate survival tactic. It's a show that just keeps on giving, no matter how many times you've watched it.

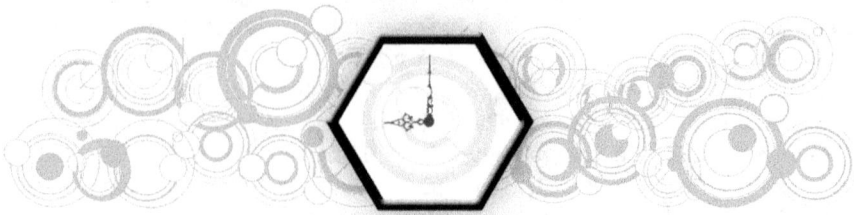

The Starlit Optimist

By Bella Farrah, aged 15, from Australia

It's twilight and the dappled golden sun dances through the open window of a little girl's room, tracing the contours of childhood on her face and whispering to her of fairytales and faraway lands. She sits, mesmerised by its song, transfixed by the scent of adventure lingering in the air. Then she stops. The air has shifted, tingling somehow, tensed as though waiting... but for what? Suddenly the corpuscle peace is shattered by the queerest sound, like that of a siren but at the same time somehow *other*. She races from her bedroom towards the sound, following it through the garden, past the fence, around the corner - until she hits it. A big blue box stands on the path in front of her, the light on top pulsing like the beating of an ancient heart. As she stands there, pondering this new discovery, the door creaks open, a ray of light spilling out onto the ground and then a hand, a *hand* reaches out into the fading light towards the girl. It wriggles its fingers once, an invitation. Hesitantly, she reaches back. When she is close enough to grasp, it latches on, flinging her in and locking the door. Spinning her around to face him, the owner of the hand simply smiles and says, "I know, I know. Isn't it *fantastic*!?

As you may have guessed, that girl was me. Eight year old me, the day Doctor Who returned to our screens in 2005. I'm fifteen now, a little girl on the brink of womanhood, and you know what? I don't feel a day older. Everyone remembers what it feels like to be here, standing in this twilight zone and trying to work out what you think and how you feel and who you want to be. In this time we turn both to and from our parents, our friends, and our role models. But I turn to *him*. To that mad man in a blue box, who stole my eight year old heart and took me away with him through all of time and space. He has taught me so much - like the fact that, believe it or not, bow ties are cool - and his constant wonder at every world and every creature is both an inspiration and a promise.

This is what he promises - the darkness, the madness and the light, all at once. It's easy to stumble through this life because, instead of looking straight ahead at where you want to go, you're looking all around you trying to find your feet. And then the Doctor leans down, takes your hand, and tells you that *you're so lucky you're still alive to see this beautiful world... everywhere we look, the complex magic of nature blazes before our eyes*, and you find a reason to stand tall. He carries so much hope, for a life full of adventure and wonder, and *it seems to me that there's so much more to the world than the average eye is allowed to see.* I believe, if you look hard enough, there are more wonders in this universe than you could ever have dreamt of...

So here I am. Still terrified, still clumsy, but also filled with this effervescent joy, the promise that *this is only one corner of one country on one continent on one planet that's a corner of a galaxy that's a corner of a universe that's forever growing and shrinking and creating and destroying and never remaining the same for a single millisecond, and there is so much to see.* There are over six billion of us, strange creatures that we are, stumbling around on a speck of dust. We are so small, but we are not insignificant, because we are made of stardust. There is only one of each of us, and there will never be another. That ancient man with the ever changing face has touched so many lives in so many ways.

I'm still waiting for him. I don't think I'll ever stop.

My Companion: The Doctor

By Nancy Orford, aged 21, from Canada

Sitting down with my Dad on a spring night in 2005, we were in need of something to watch following the conclusion of *Keeping Up Appearances*. Being 13 at the time, all I wanted to do was watch music videos or at least something for younger viewers that wasn't about middle-aged British people. Thankfully, I didn't win the battle for the TV remote as we landed on CBC (Canadian Broadcasting Corporation) just as a blonde girl let out a blood-curdling scream as a weird flying raptor thing appeared in the sky. The Reapers. That's all that took to have me engrossed in the Doctor Who universe.

Whether it's the writing, the music or the characterisation of the Doctor, the show has kept me captivated since that first day. Ultimately, it is these elements combined that make for a show that speaks across generations by enabling 'the possible' in all us of us. This is the gift the Doctor has brought me since 2005.

It was during David Tennant's reign that I really fell in love with the programme. Just as this era was beginning, so too was my time at high school. As a teenager, I was thoroughly captivated by the connection between the Doctor and Rose. I don't think I ever cried as much watching an episode of any show as I did during *Doomsday*. I thought no one could ever take the place of Rose, but along came Donna in *The Runaway Bride*, and I instantly liked her and the comedic edge that Catherine Tate brought to the show. I totally related to Martha as his companion - what teenager hasn't gone through the whole unrequited love drama? With me though, it just happened to be playing out on screen at the same time, which certainly helped. *"Just get out"* became great advice!

Before the fourth series aired in Canada, my family and I travelled to England for the summer where we saw the latter part of the series on repeat beginning with *Silence in the Library*. Seeing new episodes just thrilled me and travelling with Donna captivated me yet again. And a new theme song to top it off was brilliant! Being able to watch *Journey's End* in England seemed quite fitting as I watched the characters I had spent the last 5 years with go on to bigger and better things, sadly without the Doctor. Watching this episode in Canada proved a challenge as nearly 20 minutes was edited out for commercials. Sometimes it's hard being a Canadian Whovian!

Above all else, Doctor Who has brought me a love of music. Throughout these 8 years of New Who, the music of each episode has brought me such joy it is hard to put down in words. At the close of the first series, I sat distraught watching as the hologram of the Doctor told Rose to *"have a good life"* while Rose's Theme played in the background. From that moment on, the music Murray Gold has provided the series has been forever linked with my emotions as a viewer. No matter what episode, or the content within it, the music of Doctor Who has pulled on my heartstrings more than anything.

Growing up alongside the new series, the music began to take on a larger meaning for me. When I needed a pick-me-up, I played the Doctor Who theme because it reminded me that there's much more out there than the problems I was facing that day. With the death of a close friend came my obsession with *Doomsday*. With one listen, every emotion I felt was played back to me as I remembered that the Doctor had also lost a dear friend in Rose. With Martha as his companion, I could listen to her theme if I was in need of a confidence boost as the music resonated with both strength and determination for me. During those times where I felt like a nobody, the music of Series 4 would uplift me, just as the Doctor had done for Donna. To this day, I find comfort in listening to Gold's music as I remember an associated episode or a particular moment in my life. Gold's music is so perfect for Doctor Who that without even seeing an episode, the listener is able to relate to the emotions of the song and have it fit with different scenarios.

I was always known as the 'Doctor Who kid' in high school. I wrote essays about why Doctor Who was my favourite TV show (always to my teachers bewilderment), decorated my locker with Doctor Who magnets and pictures, wore my Tenth Doctor t-shirt to bring me good luck on a physics exam, and I vividly remember mentioning in geography class how it was actually the Doctor who had caused Vesuvius to erupt...

With the end of David Tennant's time as the Doctor, I was preparing to head off to university. During *The End of Time*, I watched as the characters I grew up with had left the Doctor and adjusted to life without him. I cried for the Doctor and his final words - *"I don't want to go"* - seemed to reflect my exact thoughts about leaving the familiarity I had grown up with - both within the show and my daily life. In a way, we were both regenerating.

To me, Doctor Who will be forever linked to my coming-of-age story. In a time where I felt unsure about most things in life, the show provided me with a sense of stability. The episodes and music were always there. The Doctor showed his companions what their true potential could be and instilled that same possibility within me. As I continue to watch the series, and experience the Classic stories too, I realise that this is the power of the show - to captivate the audience, no matter what age, and empower their creativity, their desire to learn and their curiosity and the joy of life.

Thanks to Christopher Eccleston, David Tennant, the writers, and Murray Gold for making me believe that if you have the courage to run, the possible paths you can take are endless.

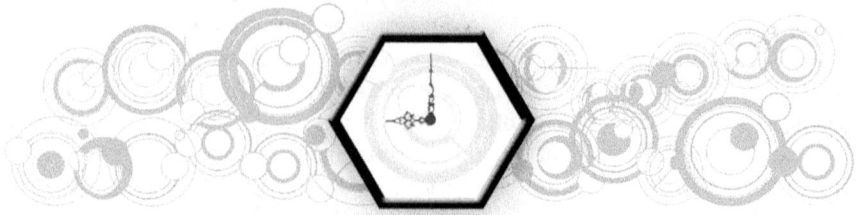

Where I Needed To Go

By Eliza Stribling, aged 18, from Australia

Like a whole lot of other people around the world, my journey with the Doctor started as a family tradition. I can still remember the first time my Dad tried to get us all to watch it - my brother ended up hidden behind the couch as Christopher Eccleston pointed his sonic screwdriver at some monster or another. We didn't watch it again for a little while after that, because we didn't want to scare him anymore, but it was from that moment that Doctor Who made its way into my, sadly, singular heart.

By 2007, the show had turned Sunday night into the one school night that we were allowed to stay up past 8 o'clock, just because Doctor Who was on. After I left the world of primary school behind me, I wandered my way into high school where the adventures I was having were apparently too good for the Doctor. I would still watch the show every week, reluctantly going along with my family as they danced to the familiar theme tune, but really, I thought I was too cool for the Doctor and all his timey-wimey madness. At least, until Matt Smith popped his head out of that smoking blue box and began to eat fish fingers and custard. I never stood a chance.

Since then, Doctor Who has become much more than just that one show about time travel and pretty people and strange looking aliens. It has been something that I can truly say I have loved wholeheartedly as it has has opened up my eyes to so many things. I would not be the person that I am today if I hadn't cried for hours over the Ponds, or dressed up as the Eleventh Doctor for three consecutive Halloweens, or pointed my store-bought Sonic Screwdriver at the sky, hoping that the Doctor or the TARDIS would hear it and appear in my backyard. It made me, a usually very by-the-book girl, get told off on a school trip for singing the 'ooo-eee-ooo' theme tune at the top of my lungs in a hotel when there were people in the next room. As a series, it has made me a better person and let me fall in love with some truly beautiful and well written characters. I am thankful to the entire cast and production team for this.

But most of all, I'm thankful for the bonds that this show has allowed me to make with people. Whether it's that old primary school friend or that girl at university with the TARDIS shirt, Doctor Who has given me the confidence to reach out and form new friendships. This show helped me to come out of my shell and show my true colours because I know that everybody is important, however seemingly insignificant. And I think most importantly, it has brought me closer to my family, giving us a weekly tradition, an excuse to mutually care about something, and a very embarrassing and slightly endearing habit of dancing whenever the show comes on...

So, thank you, Doctor Who, for being so consistently brilliant. Thank you for showing me how good I can be when I put my mind to it, and thank you for always pointing me not where I wanted to go, but where I really *needed* to go. Here's to another fifty years.

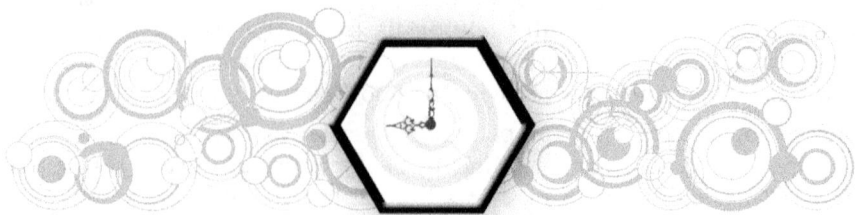

We Are All Stories

By Fanni Sütő, aged 23, from Hungary

My acquaintance with the Doctor is quite a recent one, but it has everything a good story needs: love, travel and tears. I originally come from Hungary where unfortunately Doctor Who is not as well known as it should be (but at least Martha said she had been to Budapest when looking for the secret weapon against the Master - how sad it wasn't true.) So, very fittingly, I got acquainted with Doctor Who in England during my Erasmus scholarship in London. Yep, that was the travelling part, nothing very high scale and not in the TARDIS, but good for a beginning.

I was in a very hard period of my life, one foot out from a long relationship and one foot nowhere, when I became friends with a boy who was an adamant follower of the Doctor. He, seeing that I am an intelligent looking sort of geeky girl - at least I hope that was what he saw - tried to convince me to start watching the series. I wasn't really convinced at first but as time passed and we turned into a couple and flatmates, I got converted into a Whovian. It sort of worked with me like in the well-known meme, you just sit down to check out this series everybody is talking about and next time you look up you are wearing 3D glasses, think bowties are cool and look at bananas with a different eye. We started from the modern reboot with the Ninth Doctor and watching Doctor Who became a romantic and geeky evening programme for us. The series made me cry more than all the heartbreak from cruel high school crushes - of which I had a lot - and it made me love characters as quickly and as deeply as maybe Harry Potter did. David Tennant is the most beautiful man alive and my boyfriend can't even complain because he's the one who got me addicted!

My favourite Who-related moment of all was when I returned home for the big and scary final exam of my master's program and was waiting in line with a friend of mine. While talking about different literary periods I asked her, "In which time would you like to live?" She answered: "I don't really care, as long as I can go with the TARDIS."

The Doctor - connecting people and making life better on planet Earth for fifty years.

Because of the Doctor

By Millie Salt, aged 14, from the UK

Because of the Doctor, ever since I was little I wanted to be an actress. Not for fame, not for money, but all because I wanted to be on Doctor Who. I wanted to meet the Doctor.

My love for Doctor Who started when I was five. This is when I first started watching it. I still remember the first episode I watched. It was Rose. The mannequins really scared me, but I got drawn into watching it. After that, I was hooked and I spent hours on end just sat watching Doctor Who, and I still do.

Even though I started watching Doctor Who with Christopher Eccleston, I feel that my Doctor is David Tennant. I grew up watching him. David is the Doctor I can remember sitting down and watching with my family. His easygoing yet sometimes unforgiving personality made him memorable to me and many other fans. In my eyes, David was the best.

Doctor Who has taught me a lot. It has taught me how important everyone is, it's taught me to never grow up and it's taught me to go and live a little because everyone dies so you better make the most of the time you have.

Because of the Doctor, I have tried to do that by taking every opportunity that comes my way.

Because of the Doctor.

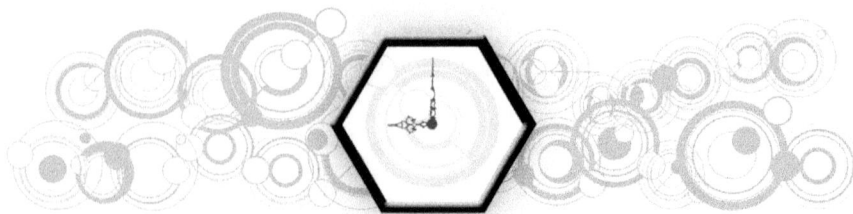

500 Miles and More

By Emma F.M, aged 34, from Spain

My adventure with the Doctor didn't start a lot of time ago. It was spring 2011, although I can't remember the specific date. My first Doctor was the Ninth. I didn't know the character and the story he had got behind him and so the early episodes I watched were very weird to me, however the Doctor seemed very funny and charming. At the same time I could relate to Rose and I understood her reactions - she was a normal girl with a boring life and suddenly a strange alien with a time machine appears. Nobody could resist to that.

I don't have an episode that I could call my favourite in this season, it might be *Father's Day* or *The Empty Child*. I experienced the regeneration of my first Doctor quickly and odd. I didn't cry then because I didn't expect it. My first reaction to the Tenth Doctor was the same that Rose had. Who are you? Where is *my* Doctor?

Poor thing, I was so naïve.

I only needed three or five episodes to accept the new Doctor. He was funnier than the Ninth and I loved his facial expressions right away. In addition, the plots of the series became better too. I LOVE the idea about the Olympics. It was the future in its premiere and now it is the past. It's awesome!

The third season was where I really discovered what Doctor Who means. I was enjoying travelling with the Doctor a lot, every adventure was different and the Tenth Doctor was very charismatic and his personality was very complex. In my opinion, the Doctor isn't a hero - he is a tormented god who sometimes is a bit arrogant, and I love this kind of character.

At this stage I started to see the world in a different way. I have always watched aliens films such as *E.T, Star Wars* and *Men in Black*, but I have never thought it could be real. It's fiction, after all, but I started to believe in the Doctor. The Doctor has inspired me in a lot in ways that I could never have imagined. I'm very happy and grateful to this.

Today I have many dreams, including to visit London, Cardiff, Scotland and meeting David Tennant. The problem is that I live in Spain and the plane ticket with a hotel is too expensive for me.

To sum up, the Doctor changed my point of view about many things and he convinces me that everything is possible to do if you believe it.

I could walk 500 miles and more with the Doctor.

Whovianism: Your Guide to Living Life

By Chew Wei Li, aged 18, from Singapore

I'm not as qualified as a lot of others, I think, to be writing this, as I've only started watching Doctor Who from its 2005 revival, albeit finding some of the Classic Doctor Who episodes too. Nevertheless, even within such a short time - relative to the whole show - of watching, it's just affected me more deeply than any show I've ever watched or ever will. It's more than a show, it's like a life philosophy, a religion, a guidebook to life. Many people will scoff at this and say it's all just fiction, but often, fiction doesn't just reflect reality, it illuminates it. It changes how we view it, how we deal with it, how we live it. This is what Doctor Who has done for me, and I feel I've learnt plenty from it. Throughout my own experience watching Doctor Who, it hasn't just been the fascinating, mind bending sci-fi adventure one may think it to be, but it has provided me with someone whose attitude, outlook and character I will continually be inspired by and aspire towards: The Doctor.

For one, there is a great deal of positivity one can learn and gain from him. And the next time a Whovian falls, he'll learn to just pick himself up, straighten his bow tie and put on a smile. The Doctor has taught me that life is a pile of good things and bad things, and we shouldn't just mull over the bad things all the time. And though he makes us realise that we can't ever run away from our past without it ever catching up once in a while, we learn a balance. We learn to run from it yet learn from it, to not think about it yet not forget it, to not let it restrict us yet let it put us in our places. We live the rest of our lives fully, we don't let it get us down, but we never, ever forget it. Doctor Who has made me realise the value of past mistakes and regrets, and how to live with them to the best.

The Doctor has also taught me the power of empathy, of mutual understanding, and of peace. He taught me that violence begets violence and does not solve it. Many times I've marvelled at, then smiled at, the power of non-violence in the show. But it also made me take note of the countless times this happened in reality, despite the common perception that, as harsh as it sounds, non-violence accomplishes nothing in the real world. When everyone else forgot the times when it did, I think Whovians remembered. Because it brought that same smile to their faces. I think I will always stand by the power of peace. Countless times too, the show has reminded me that each individual, each race, each species or planet has its own interests, and are very much like us. It has taught me tolerance, and mutual understanding. It has shamed many of us, when we assumed non-humans to be our immediate enemy and threat, later to realise that they were just like us, if not better.

Doctor Who has made me more able to handle situations of conflict or misunderstanding, as I realised that often it was simply a matter of changing perspectives, or seeing the other side. Of course, they teach us all this in school or whatnot, but who actually listens unless it's in the form of Doctor Who, really?

Another thing I've learnt from Doctor Who is how important, and how powerful, loyalty can be. More than courage, or intellect, or physical strength. There are so many times we've been moved to tears in the show by the immense loyalty of its characters to one another. And loyalty doesn't have to be giving one's life up - maybe several times - to save someone else, or waiting 2,000 years alone outside a box just to protect someone, or giving up marriage, or giving up a life you could have had just to help or be with that someone... Whatever it is, Doctor Who has made me realise the importance of never walking away, never walking out on the people you care about. And this is so often much more powerful than one's aptitude.

In addition to all this big serious stuff, I've learnt not to take myself and my life's chronicles too seriously, because what I am and what I have is just a speck of what's out there, in all of space and time. It's made me appreciate not just my life and what it revolves around, but appreciate the world, the universe. Though fictional, it makes us see how far we've come - and how far we've yet to go - as a species. And if one tiny thing happened differently, how an entire future could be changed. Its glimpses into the possible universe leave no space for cynicism, because who can prove that there isn't, somewhere out there, a world where the laws of our reality don't exist? It's revealed to me how much could be out there, inspiring hope and beauty, curiosity and humility, as I lift my eyes skyward every night. At the same time, it's made me realise that in all our tiny little ways, we can make a difference, and that in all of time and space there's not one single person who isn't important. As much as our lives are one thin thread in the fabric of reality, each thread is closely interwoven with the others, such that each tiny unit of life is responsible to a much larger cohesive whole. No one is trapped in the ordinary, and anyone can be, and is part of, something great.

This, among so many more reasons, is why such a dear old show can become more than a show, but a philosophy, a religion, a "guide to life" handbook. And this is why I love it.

The Girl Who Changed Her Mind

By Alexandra, aged 15, from the US

Science fiction was not my thing. I have always been paranoid about aliens and bored out of my mind watching fantasy films. My real story begins, however, that one night at the fast food joint...

All my friends had great excitement as they conversed around the table. I picked up a few of the many words they spoke of. Daleks, The Doctor, and Screwdrivers. I eventually spoke up.

"What are you all talking about?" I asked eagerly.

My friends ooked at each other and my friend Kate leaned towards me. The whiff of her breath grazed my nose.

"Nothing that would interest you. You wouldn't like it all, Alexandra."

She turned her back to me and looked in the other direction. I quickly became very curious. That evening I typed 'The Doctor' into my computer. Then came up the answer I was waiting for. I knew I had to watch this. After turning down every show in the same genre, something in me wanted to see it. I would soon learn that the Doctor is in a genre of his own.

I began to watch *Rose* which I found very enjoyable. I was slightly confused at first, however after a few minutes it was this confusion that now made me adore the show so much. The confusion became excitement and mystery. I started watching more episodes with Matt Smith and he quickly became my favourite. He was my Doctor! The way he talked, moved and even smiled. I soon found myself watching more and more episodes. I could not get enough. I began watching the show in every second I was free. When I wasn't free it was because I was watching an Amy Pond makeup tutorial or painting the TARDIS on my fingernails!

The Trip of a Lifetime

By Eva, aged 16, from the UK

Sometime in early 2005, a member of my family switched the radio on. I have an appalling memory, and most of my life pre-2011 is a little fuzzy, but this particular moment I remember quite vividly. As I entered the kitchen I was met with the sight of both my parents listening with an unusual level of engagement to the interview on the radio. A mancunian man was chatting to one of the usual radio DJs, about his new TV show. The show was called Doctor Who.

"What's Doctor Who?" I asked, bemused by my parents' level of interest in something mundane as a radio interview.

My father turned to me and began to explain. It was all a bit of a blur and I'm sure my face wore the same expression I myself am met with when explaining to people who are unfamiliar with it, what exactly the concept of Britain's best loved TV show is. The bit a do remember from his explanation was, *"...and it's had the same theme song for 40 years"*.

On the Saturday 2nd April 2005, having much to my despair missed episode one, Rose, being on holiday, myself and the three other members of my family sat down on our sofa, in front of our old second-hand TV, and watched Doctor Who Series 1, Episode 2, *The End of the World*. It didn't take me long to become utterly and completely enthralled by the Doctor, Rose and his time traveling box. Back at school, nobody was talking about anything else.

Since that day I've jumped on the proverbial bandwagon for the latest trend many times, but I've never completely forgotten the Doctor. This quote from a recent issue of Doctor Who magazine sums up my point quite eloquently:

"The difference between a craze and a passion, however, is that passion endures. For many of us, Doctor Who is always there, underneath, long after temporary devotion to Rubik's cubes or the Spice Girls or Tamagotchis has faded away."

No matter what, when all the excitement had blown over, and the hype had faded, the Doctor would still be there waiting to promise me *"the trip of a lifetime"*.

The Never Ending Fandom

By Evan Barr, aged 12, from Alberta, Canada

For some people, Doctor Who started with the Classics, during the Hartnelll era. For me, Doctor Who was an accident. It was any other day in my house, with my Dad, my brother, and my sister. I was maybe nine. Nothing important was happening. But then, my Dad decides to turn on the television, and brings up a new show none of us had ever seen before. Doctor Who.

My Dad always wants us kids to *"open our minds to new things"*, and he's right. We should. But Doctor Who was nothing out of my comfort zone. He turned on episode one of the new series. That's right, the Ninth Doctor. Instantly, I was baffled by it. Living plastic, a time machine made from wood, and the Doctor! He was eccentric, funny, like a child on screen. After that, I was hooked. So we watched more episodes. They kept getting better and better. Daleks, ghosts, the Earth's fiery destruction. They were amazing. So we watched more. My sister got a little bored of it. Too bad she didn't stay around for the Tennant era. My favourite Doctor, to be honest.

Forget how much I watched the show, I went all over the place. I bought Sonic screwdrivers, TARDIS cookie jars, books, basically everything I could find (and afford). Harry Potter ended after I finished the books (four times), but Doctor Who will never die for me. Even now, with no new episodes left, and the frustration of having to wait until late November, Doctor Who will never die. It is the never ending fandom.

My Childhood with the Doctor

By Leanne Wells, aged 17, from the UK

It was 2nd April 2005 when I stumbled across Doctor Who. I was 8 days away from my 9th birthday when I saw the last 10 minutes of The End of the World. Shamefully, I wasn't that interested in Doctor Who when I first saw it, however, 8 months later I saw *The Christmas Invasion* on Christmas Day and I was well and truly hooked. Every Saturday night was Doctor Who night from then on. Each episode was followed by Doctor Who Confidential on BBC Three and that was a must for any true Whovian.

The Tenth Doctor was, and still is, my Doctor. I spent five wonderful years with the him going on many adventures and learning about history and science too. But on 29th October 2008, I remember crying for many, many hours. During the *National Television Awards*, David Tennant announced that he was leaving Doctor Who.

Despite my devastation, not once did I regret becoming a Whovian. The community is so warm and supportive that we all cried together when the Doctor and Rose were separated, and then again when the Tenth Doctor regenerated.

Without Doctor Who, my childhood wouldn't have been so good. My childhood was nerdy and full of 'in jokes'. I have lots of memories of scribbling *'Bad Wolf'* in random places and I always carried a key around in my pocket so when the TARDIS materialised in front of me, I'd be able to unlock the doors and disappear off to a foreign land with the Doctor. I must admit, I still hope for that blue box to appear on a street corner...

I can't wait until the 50th anniversary episode and it'll be great to see David and Billie again after so long. So thank you Doctor Who, for making my childhood, as the Ninth Doctor would say, *"fantastic"*. I know more about history and science than school could ever hope to teach and I have a vast array of phrases and quotes that often don't make sense but can be used in most situations anyway.

Thank you to Russell T Davies, Mark Gatiss, Steven Moffat, Toby Whithouse, Tom MacRae, Matt Jones, Matthew Graham, Gareth Roberts, Helen Raynor, Stephen Greenhorn, Chris Chibnall, Paul Cornell, James Moran, Keith Temple and Phil Ford for writing for the Tenth Doctor. Without your imaginative, terrifying and exciting stories, I wouldn't have fallen in love with Doctor Who.

And finally, thank you to David Tennant, Billie Piper, John Barrowman, Freema Agyeman, Catherine Tate, Christopher Eccleston (for those ten minutes in April 2005!), Julie Gardner and Phil Collinson. Without these brilliant people, I wouldn't have lived the dream for so long!

So onwards and upwards to the 50th anniversary, the 75th anniversary and the 100th anniversary. Doctor Who, I'm sure, will live forever.

That Mad Man in a Box

By Audrey Stadler, aged 17, from the USA

Doctor Who. Doctor who?

This question, about three years ago, didn't really mean much to me. I lived a pretty uneventful life. Well, by 'uneventful' I mean that I wasn't afraid of random statues, I could walk in shadows, I didn't fear every robot was going to kill me and I thought every number on a clock was just a number! I was always curious, though. Who was this Doctor and why did everyone like him so much?

Some of my friends at school were pretty big fans. They talked about Doctor Who a lot and to be honest, I hated not knowing what they were talking about. One summer before my sophomore year of high school in my pretty uneventful life, that all changed.

In Southeast America, it's way too hot to go outside in the summer. You only go outside when you're forced to, either as an obligation to sports or to take out the trash. Around noon on one of those days, I was lucky enough to not be obligated to either, so I did what every teenager did. I turned on the TV.

I was never committed to a show before and I never dedicated myself to one. I didn't know what it was like to cry over characters or have anticipation for the next episode. Again, my life was pretty uneventful. I was scrolling through the On Demand listings when, to peak my interest, Doctor Who came up as one of the suggestions. Thinking to myself, *"Let's see what all the fuss is all about..."*, I clicked on the first episode. And that is when my life changed forever.

That first episode alone got me into the series. It was weird and exciting and like nothing I had never seen before. Then again, where else would you see shop window dummies coming to life on your TV? Out of sheer boredom of my uneventful life and the excitement of this show, I kept watching. The Ninth Doctor - despite his really big ears and nose - had an impression on me. He was witty, charming, and sarcastic. And then came 10.

David Tennant will always be one of my favorite actors and his portrayal of the Tenth Doctor definitely made me fall in love with the series. I can't even describe Tennant's Doctor because that would be like describing how to exterminate to a Dalek. You just can't! David Tennant changed the series forever. David Tennant changed *Whovians* forever.

Speaking of Whovians, you can't really understand what it's like to be a Whovian unless you watch the show and become one. It's that shared connection with random strangers, that fear of inanimate objects, and that love for a man with two hearts that brings a community together. To me, being a Whovian is so much more than just the show. It's about becoming part of a family you didn't even realise you had. You can go up to anyone with a Doctor Who shirt or accessory and just have a conversation about the space-time continuum!

On 23rd November 1963, I don't think anyone could have predicted that Doctor Who would have such a huge impact. Over 50 years, it has brought generations together. Doctor Who has influenced cultures, scientific studies and even the world to be open to the possible idea of a mad man in a box. 50 years ago, did anyone think it was possible for a kid in Russia and a kid in America to watch the same show and become friends through that show via the Internet? It is a radical idea that so many people around the world, from so many backgrounds and cultures, can come together to obsess over one mad man, one blue box and 50 years of what is one of the greatest shows the world has ever seen.

Doctor Who has even brought my own personal family together. I can now talk to my sisters, who also watch the show, about anything, Doctor Who related or not. We have built a connection that wasn't there before, one that Doctor Who helped to make. I can't really imagine my life without Doctor Who now. Before it, I didn't realise what it was like to be truly passionate about something. Before Doctor Who, I did not live.

And Doctor Who is still growing and expanding. With the 50th anniversary around the corner, the world will be celebrating half a century of unity, family, crying, laughing, excitement and, of course, that mad man in a box.

The Most Wonderful Man in the Universe

By David Scott, aged 26, from the UK

Looking back now, I can see I always was, and I use the term very fondly, a 'geek'. As a child, if I liked something, such as a television show, I didn't just like it, I knew everything I could about it. Even as a teenager I had action figures (not toys!) that I was far too old for. Not to play with, but just because they looked cool. Of course, that's not how everyone else saw it. Despite what I thought, it wasn't cool to show off your massive collection of *Power Rangers* toys or *Pokémon* drawings. Very quickly, all of these things became something I kept to myself, hidden away in my bedroom.

It's obvious now that I was an archetypal Doctor Who fan, the stereotypical obsessive, custom made to embrace the show, its history, and everything about it. However, there was a problem with that, a rather unavoidable one which made it rather difficult for me to embrace my inevitable passion for the show. I was born in 1986.

Although Doctor Who ran for a further three years, neither of my parents were fans at the time (although I'd later find out that my Dad saw all of the Hartnell era, and remembers his despair when his Doctor regenerated), so as far as I knew, the show didn't exist. Even in 1996 I managed to miss the TV movie, probably because I just wasn't interested.

My first real memory of Doctor Who is when I was 15. I must have known of the show as when on holiday in Wales with my Dad and sister, and given the choice of visiting a Doctor Who museum (sign posted by a Dalek on a tourist sign), or yet another military exhibition, I picked the former immediately. I think my plan had been to feign some interest, just to get through another rainy afternoon, but as soon as I walked through the door to be greeted by a Cyberman looming over me, I was hooked. I remember spending hours wandering around, taking in the different monsters and props, including the TARDIS, something which would become so iconic to me a few years later. This was around 2001, and I had no idea that Doctor Who would be coming back, let alone become such a big part of my life. Granted, I enjoyed the visit, but at the time it had no lasting impact on me, as there was nothing to fuel my interest. We were on a caravanning holiday, so I couldn't just jump online and '*Ask Jeeves*' to tell me more about Doctor Who (I don't think I'd discovered the joy of *Google* yet). Instead, by the time we had gotten home, I'd forgotten about Doctor Who completely.

Despite have no real extended exposure to Doctor Who, I remember knowing that I wanted to watch the show when its relaunch was announced in 2005. I was, once again, on a caravanning holiday, but this time things were much different. My parents were now divorced, my sister lived with our mother and no longer holidayed with us either. I'd finished my GCSEs and was doing my A-Levels, having suddenly been thrown into a grown up world where I had much more to worry about than collecting action figures. On the Saturday afternoon my Dad and I had fallen out, an argument over my Mum, who was not so conveniently on holiday with her new partner just down the road. It wasn't a good time in general, let alone a good holiday. But still, over dinner in the caravan, on that Saturday night in April, we sat down and watched Doctor Who together. My first episode. I've always wondered, but never asked, if that had meant anything to Dad, particularly since learning that that he watched the very first episode in 1963 with his own father, who had passed away only a few years before.

I think there was something more than shouting at aliens and travelling through time that drew me to the character of the Doctor. He was angry. Not just on the outside, but all the way through. That's just the way I was feeling too. So angry at everyone and everything, thrown in the middle of a situation that I hadn't planned to be in. Unfortunately, that's where the similarities ended. The Doctor could do something about it, whereas I was stuck with the cards I'd been dealt. That didn't mean I couldn't try and run away though. Not literally though. Oh no, my next stop? *The End of the World*.

Then we got to Dalek, the episode that changed my view on the show with one chilling scene. I knew what Daleks were, their catchphrase, their dislike of stairs, but it wasn't the lone alien that moved me. It was the Doctor, screaming pure hatred at the defenceless creature locked in the cell. There he was, the character I'd seen as being able to hide away all of that pain and loneliness, letting all of his emotions out and torturing another being because it made him feel better. And that's when I realised. It's OK to be upset and angry. We all have things that eat us up inside, whether it be your parents divorcing, or having to wipe out your entire race in order to stop an eternal war. If the Doctor could cry at facing his demons, so could I. And I did.

What I've realised whilst writing this is that in a relatively short time, this little television show has had such an impact on me, so the same must apply to so many other people in this country, and beyond. To everyone else outside of Doctor Who, this all means nothing. It's about me and a show about a mad man in a box. But to me it's a massive part of my life, and I'm sure there are people out there who can relate. In the long run, it doesn't matter. None of what I've written does, it's just the story of me and Doctor Who.

Because, after all, we're all just stories in the end.

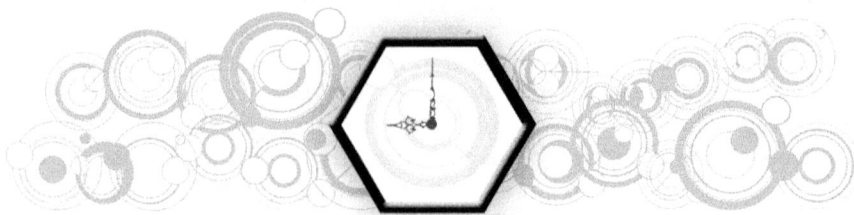

The Moment I Met the Doctor

By Megan Reeves, aged 20, from the UK

My Doctor Who journey began at the tender age of 12 years old. My mother was always A Doctor Who fan, religiously following Pertwee and Troughton's era in particular. As I was growing up, she used to tell me stories about how she used to hide behind her sofa and under a cushion, yet still peeking through her hands despite being terrified. *"They call them Daleks"* she'd say to me. To me, though, they sounded pretty silly from the description - *"a whisk and plunger"?* - but I was a young and foolish child. Little did I know, over a decade later, I would be hiding behind the same sofa my mother did all those years ago...

Being born in 1993, in what we like to call 'The Wilderness Years', I had the privilege of being properly introduced to Doctor Who when it was rebooted in 2005. Now being just 12 (my birthday was a couple of weeks before), I didn't really know what to expect. Yes, I had my mother's stories but that was her. Something like that might not appeal to me, right? Wrong.

It was a rainy day in my hometown of Essex. I had just been given a small television for my bedroom (the thrill! My *own remote*!) and, whilst watching BBC One, I suddenly heard a *BOOMING* drum beat and a dark and thrilling tune burst onto my cheap television.

"Do you wanna come with me?" This tall, big eared, leather clad man told me. *"You'll see all sorts of things."* My eyes and ears immediately opened wide with intrigue and delight. The launch trailer of the show featured this 'Doctor', running dramatically down a curiously long corridor away from a blazing trail of fire in slow motion. My mouth slowly dropped as it progressed. I had so many questions already. What's that machine that's making those noises? Why does he have such big ears!? The montage of what was to be expected whizzed past my eager eyes. Was that Big Ben!? To top it off, a girl appeared at the end. She was pretty and feisty looking. Hold up a minute, it was only Billie Piper, whose music I'd followed years before!

From that point on, I was sold. I knew I *had* to watch it, and I am so glad I did. 8 years later, now at the not so tender age of 20, I can safely say that Doctor Who has changed my life. Watching the "New Who" made me want to watch the Classic era, which is equally as brilliant and equally as emotional. I love the fact that the show still has the same morals and foundations that were built 50 years ago.

I am completely and irrevocably in love with the show, and I wouldn't have it any other way. To some it might be just a TV show, but to me and millions of others, it's a way of life.

Allons-y!

By Amber Jackson, aged 14, from the UK

My adventure with the Doctor began when I was 7. I was a latecomer to the show's reboot in 2005 so, in 2006, my Dad sat me down to watch the repeats of Christopher Eccleston's episodes.

I instantly fell in love with the show and the Doctor. At this point half of Series 2 had aired on TV so I spent the rest of my time watching Series 1 and catching up with Series 2. This is where my love for the show really kicked in. This is where I met my Doctor, the Tenth Doctor, played by David Tennant.

David was the perfect Doctor to watch whilst growing up. He was an inspiration because of his sense of throwing himself into any and every situation. I loved his ability to talk at 1000 miles an hour, his determination, and his witty and cheeky manners, yet at the same time his vengeful and unforgiving side.

I'm writing this 5 days after Peter Capaldi was announced as the Twelfth Doctor. At first I wasn't sure about the choice but I think that's all because I'm still upset about Matt leaving. I saw him in *The Fires of Pompeii* and *Torchwood: Children of Earth* and I now believe that it's going to be a good change to have an older Doctor. I just want to wish Peter the best of luck. I know he's going to be amazing! I also want to wish Matt the best of luck - he was an absolutely fantastic Doctor and I'm sure he'll do great with his future acting jobs.

So, to that madman with a box who made bow ties cool...

"Geronimo!"

T'was the Night Before Christmas

By Richard Nobbe, aged 20, from the Netherlands

I recall my first encounter with the Doctor. It was a particularly dull Christmas evening in my tiny, Dutch home. My Dad, slightly irritable because of the really bad game shows shown on Dutch TV, decided to set the TV on BBC One. This was an odd choice - we never watched the BBC. It was this odd show about a man (who, according to my Dad, had a ridiculously long scarf the last time he saw him)whizzing about in a blue box which somehow was bigger on the inside. A twelve year old me was captivated by the strange, strange adventures of this silly man who was able to re-grow his hand after it had been cut off by a sword-wielding Sycorax. My poor grasp of the English language at the time reduced the text so brilliantly uttered by the actors to a big, steaming pile of mumbo-jumbo which I quite frankly enjoyed.

Fast forward six years. Me, being the bored out of my mind, introverted teenager I am, searches the Internet for a new series to watch, I search, skipping loads of not-quite-as-impressive shows until I land on the image of a blue box, a blue box which, vaguely settled in my memory, reminded me of that one Christmas evening. At the very moment the Ninth Doctor opened his mouth and uttered the now famous word "Run', I was hooked.

I lived the Doctor's life, following him through all his hardships and victories, his sad losses and his moments of bliss as I tried to read up on the massive back stories of the silly, scarf-wearing-in-the-past Time Lord. Two years later, although I am a very fanatic reader, I am still not finished on reading up on the fifty years of history of one of the deepest characters in television history.

Over the years the Doctor has - ironically, since he's an alien - shown the essence of being a human being. Or at least shown the essence of what a human being should be like. We should all try to help others when we can, whether we know them, don't know them or even when they're from an alien planet. We should love the ones who deserve to be loved, and try to love the ones who don't. We should all be ourselves, and if that includes an accent from the North, a mild French vocabulary or a preference for bow ties, so be it. Everybody needs a Doctor in their lives, and we should all strive to be that Doctor for at least one person. The Doctor taught me to be *human*.

And if ever that silly blue box lands on the corner of my tiny, little Dutch street, I won't hesitate one bit.

Next stop: *everywhere*.

Abandoning Reality to Source the Truth

By Amy McLean, aged 21, from the UK

I'd never suggest that I didn't enjoy it, but I'd reached an age where playing with toys had become a mere echo of my past. Gone were the days when I could spend Christmas morning littering the carpet with wooden train tracks, or spend hours dressing up dolls in festive outfits. No, I'd been a teenager for just short of a year. I was growing up. I was growing up, and I didn't like it.

I needed an escape.

The television schedule in December is always colourful, so I knew I'd be able to lose myself in some show or another in the evening. However, nothing could have prepared me for the adventure upon which I was about to embark.

After flicking aimlessly through the channels I crash-landed on BBC. In an instant it seemed to be trying to hypnotise me as an array of lights flashed across the screen. And then there was the mysterious blue box. If for no reason other than curiosity, I decided to stay tuned.

I was stunned. An hour later my jaw had dropped to the floor, my eyes piercing wide. It had happened the moment he had pressed that "great big threatening button". My heart had exploded, dividing itself into a million tiny fragments to be scattered across the galaxies. Who was this strange man wearing pyjamas? Why does he have two hearts? And, more importantly, how did he manage to make his hair so *perfect*? The answer, I soon learned, was simple. He was the Doctor.

He was *my* Doctor.

I was hooked. Time travel had become my sustenance, space filtered through my every breath. I'd managed to rattle out the contents of my piggy bank and pull together the requirements to travel with the Ninth Doctor. My heart raced with every adventure. Together we chased the Slitheen, fought off the Reaper, confronted the Daleks. I had become at one with the TARDIS. I felt like I had been reborn, living in a world where I knew I belonged.

But before I knew it, I was faced with my greatest challenge yet. My soul had been torn down the middle and forced to separate into two different universes. The Doctor on one side, Rose on the other. The tears streamed down my face as I fought for an answer that would solve this unbearable heartache.

I had forgotten about real existence. I didn't want it. I didn't *need* it. I had one mission in life: I must travel with the Doctor. But there was something I had to do first. I knew he wouldn't come to me in this unsightly state. I had to find perfection.

I thought it would be easy. I sought inspiration in the words of his companion. She had been down this road. She would be able to offer wisdom. I knew I wasn't yet good enough for the Doctor. I wasn't what he wanted, but if I tried to be more like his companions, more like those who had achieved success, he would come and find me.

With each day I allowed myself to believe that I was on the route to the elusive state of perfection. It started quite innocent, with a skipped meal and the odd jog through the park. I knew I would soon be exploring with the Doctor, and everything would be resolved..

The unforeseen spiral down which I soon plummeted, however, sharply put an end to my imminent satisfaction.

I ran. I purged. I starved. I had to become pure for the Doctor to love me. But I had a fight on my hands. I was battling my own creature, and this was something that was to prove a greater challenge than any Sycorax or Krillitane or Dalek could bring.

My organs were shutting down. I had pushed my body to the limit. I didn't have much time. If the Doctor was with me, he could save me. He could take me back in time, back to before I had lost control of my own existence. When had that been? It was hard to tell. My self-suppression had veiled me from any real sense of time. I needed help, I knew I did, but I had pushed everyone away. The blackness of reality tried to force itself down upon me, suffocating me as I fought to find a way out.

I had been on the edge of giving up. I was unable to comprehend this tangible world around me. It was there, and I was not. I didn't know where I was, or where I belonged.

As Bannakaffalatta ran across the screen, however, I began to understand the ability to intertwine two worlds. Two years had passed since I first locked eyes on the Doctor, and now I sat in my hospital bed with my eyes glued to the television, desperately trying to salvage that last ray of hope from the Christmas Special. As I should have predicted, just before it was too late, the Doctor saved the day.

As I lay there, exhausted and frail, the realisation began to grow inside of me. The Doctor wouldn't want me in this condition. I was too weak to help him. Not only had reality become impossible, but my condition had rendered fantasy an unbearable state of existence. Something had to change.

I vowed from that day that I would not sink any further. I would, instead, soar above any difficulties that arose, casting them into the shadows of my past with the understanding that perfection does not exist. It took me a long time to realise that, but had I not been encouraged to stray down the darkness of time, I would not know the truth, the truth that nobody needs to change who they are, physically or mentally, in order to impress somebody else. The Doctor, I now know, would not appreciate such falseness, and the same goes for our own conventional realm.

The Doctor took me on the ultimate adventure of self-discovery, a necessary action for building courage and determination. Nobody is perfect. The Doctor is not perfect. But everybody has their values.

It doesn't need to be said that Doctor is darker and more dangerous than first meets the eye. It's becoming knowledge that everybody in his path will suffer at some point. But all is not flawed, as, without him, where would we be? Above all of his offerings, the Doctor teaches us to spread our wings. He provides us with the passion, love and compassion required to grow into the very people we were born to be.

Thank you, Doctor

By Laura López Lamiel, aged 25, from Spain

I remember very vividly the first time I saw the Doctor. It was 2009 and I wasn't in my finest moment. I was very sad. I wanted to smile but I couldn't. One night and by chance, I saw a man on my TV who captured my attention. He was wearing a brown suit with a long coat and that hair. I didn't know him, but for some reason I knew he was a very special man.

I didn't know it yet, but that night was the beginning of my story with the Doctor. Specifically, the Tenth Doctor and his lovely companion Rose Tyler. Every night I turned the television on to see his adventures and I became a huge fan of the show. One of the most beautiful things that happened to me was that, thanks to the show, I smiled again. I don't know how but that charismatic, crazy, clever and goofy man made me smile every time I saw him. I forgot my problems thanks to him and for 45 minutes I travelled to different places to meet new friends and enemies.

When the Tenth Doctor regenerated into the Eleventh I felt devastated. My Doctor wasn't there anymore. I felt so attached to this character that I didn't know what to think about the new Doctor. I thought I would never watch the show again, but I was so wrong. David Tennant is and always will be my Doctor, but Matt Smith is awesome as well. It's very funny but the Doctor changed when I changed. The Tenth Doctor was there for me when I was sad and he helped me to smile again and the Eleventh Doctor is with me in a different phase of my life. Now I'm happy again and many things have changed in my life, but something remains the same: the Doctor.

The main character of this show is an alien from Gallifrey but I think Doctor Who is about us. The Doctor is a character that shows humans their virtues. He wants to help us to believe in ourselves. It's a show about optimism and hope because impossible is nothing. We have to confront our fears and be strong because we can be amazing. Absolutely amazing. I think this is the Doctor's message.

The Doctor rescued me when I wasn't happy and didn't believe in a better life. He may be a lonely traveller but there are many people around the world waiting for him. This wonderful man who travels across the stars has been with me all this time and for that I am extremely grateful. When I recovered, a new Doctor took my hand and I've been travelling with him ever since then.

The Doctor Who Saved Me

By Foram D, aged 23, from India

It is only recently that I came across the show Doctor Who, a few months back to be more precise, and it would not be an exaggeration when I say that the show saved me. People who have never watched Doctor Who would roll their eyes at this, muttering to themselves, "She has gone utterly bonkers - how can a mere TV show *save* someone?". But people who have watched the show will ne nodding in agreement, speechless, for they themselves will have experienced the same thing.

If you ask how, the answer is not simple. However, I would like to explain. Last year I suffered a terrible loss, one that ripped me to my very soul, and still comes to haunt me occasionally when I divulge into my vault of memories. I was so very lonely, almost self-destructive, angry and hopeless almost all of the time. I treated my family badly, was cruel to my best of friends, and hated myself for it all. I watched a lot of TV shows, just to keep my mind occupied, but none of them really touched me deeply.

Last month I discovered Doctor Who and I have not been the same since. The show has taught me that there is so much more out there than personal suffering, and sometimes the best way to deal with one's pain is to experience the pain of others. How the Doctor tirelessly travels across universes, saving lives, never for one fraction of a second giving up on his duties inspires you, making you want to become a better and more compassionate person. Come to think of it, they are not really his duties. He can choose to merely travel and be a spectator, but he chooses to help, to make someone else's issues his own, and to do the best that he can to sort them out.

The Doctor taught me that the simplest of human beings is worth rescuing, and everyone is important, no matter how small or insignificant he or she may seem. The Doctor taught me that everyone deserves a chance. Even when he is out there trying to stop the baddies, he gives them a choice, a second chance to retreat and mend their ways.

The Doctor taught me that sometimes loving someone means knowing exactly when to let go and say goodbye. It is not about endless time spent together, but spending the time together so well and cherishing the memories that you shared. He taught me how to forgive. The Master treated the Doctor so badly, but in the end the Doctor forgave him. That takes strength, unlike seeking

I know I am sounding like I am giving out a sermon, but these are the little and important things in life that we people forget to implement so often that we end up leading destructive lives. The Doctor rescued me from becoming an irreversibly bitter person, got me out of the trance of self-loathing. The show has taught me more about life than any religious book out there, and for that I will always be grateful.

Thank you, Doctor, for I was so very alone and so self-destructive. You brought me out of that and I owe you so much.

The Ordinary Girl

By Jessi Olivia Cadenhead, aged 18, from Guatemala

I gulped the last bite of my juicy steak, slouched back and felt as if I was in heaven. I looked over at my best friend who was still finishing up her dinner, as well as her parents. I absolutely loved their British culture, food, accents, everything. Little did I know that they would soon introduce me to something British that I would like even more than all those put together...

When my friend and I were done we took our food over to sink in the kitchen and rinsed them out. While I was waiting for her to finish rinsing her dishes, I took a look around. It had been almost four years since I'd been back in this house, and though some few obvious changes were there, it was still the same. I looked at the fridge, and noticed a magnet that had always been there, but that I had never really looked at before. There was a tall thin man with a determined look on his face. He wore Converse and a blue pin-stripe suit.

"Who is this?" I asked my friend as she finished her dishes. She walked over.

"Oh, that's the Doctor," she replied. "He's from the television show Doctor Who."

I had always heard of the show, just as one always hears of anything with a cult following. I had some friends that watched the show and sometimes talked about it. I even vaguely remembered watching an episode back in 2005 with my Mom. But I didn't remember this guy at all.

I was intrigued, so my friend showed me a book she had all about this "Doctor". She briefed me on the history of her Doctor, of his companions who travelled through time and space with him. We sat down and watched an episode with cat nuns in a futuristic hospital. It was genius! Romantic, sad, exciting, funny and weird all at once. I was immediately hooked.

After that summer I went home to my family who were currently living in Central America. Even though it was going to be a busy school year, every night I would plop down on my couch and watch Doctor Who on *Netflix*. I even managed to keep my grades up and not only did I have fun watching it, I was able to become better friends and even make new ones.

Sometimes I question what the big deal about Doctor Who is, even why I love it, what made it different from any other science fiction show. Then as I was watching it and I realised. I could relate to these human companions. A lot of shows have interesting characters, but many of them have super human abilities, or just skills above the average human in general. But with Doctor

Who it shows completely normal, everyday people having amazing adventures, falling in love, saving the world, or even rescuing all of creation. I love this show not only because of the daydreams, the friendship, or the cool effects. I love it because it encourages normal people, like me, to be better people, to be fearless, to do great things. Because we are completely capable.

It All Started With a Dalek

By Jenna Ward, aged 37, from Scotland, UK

If someone had told me 10 years ago that I would soon be married to an English man, living in Scotland with two kids, and in love with the longest running sci-fi show ever... well we all know the answer to that cliché. But looking back on the last few years of my life I ask the question, "what would my life be without Doctor Who?" I simply for the life of me could not imagine. For the last four years it seems like I have eaten, slept and breathed Doctor Who. And it all started with a Dalek.

I found this remote controlled Dalek that spoke and was at the time about as big as my son Tadd. I thought it would be a fun toy. Little did I know that single toy would shape and mould him into the biggest Doctor Who fan EVER. At the time of purchasing the Dalek, I wasn't too familiar with the show as it was not too popular in the States when I was growing up. But I moved to Scotland in 2005 when the show was reborn and the toys were available everywhere. By the time my son was two, we had started watching the odd (not too be confused with *Ood*) show here and there with David Tennant as the Doctor. As the saying goes, you never forget your first Doctor. The more we watched as a family, the more Tadd and I fell in love with the show.

It was at the end of David's run as the Doctor that our adventures started taking off. Matt Smith and Karen Gillan were touring around the UK to promote the new series and we were able to meet them in Inverness. Tadd showed Matt his sonic, and Matt bent down beside his stroller and showed him the new sonic that opened up. Matt was so sweet, we immediately accepted him as the new Doctor and it made the transition easier as David stepped down. From there it is all a whirlwind. From the Doctor Who live show in Glasgow (I was very pregnant), to the Doctor who Experience in London and Cardiff, conventions, museum exhibits, to the birth of my second son who had heard the music while in my belly and could be soothed to sleep by it, it was clear to see we were a 100% Whovian family.

Being a Whovian in our household goes way beyond sitting as a family and watching the show on a Saturday night. It starts from the moment the boys wake up, playing with the toys, dressing up, watching the Classics, drawing and making up their own stories, telling Knock Knock Doctor Who jokes, and gaining nicknames that will last a lifetime. Kirk, my youngest, was called K-9 from birth by Tadd. Daddy tends to be from UNIT since he was in the RAF for many years, and various other family members portrayed assistants and enemies (such as Uncle Foo as Doctor Tom because of his curly hair, nanny as Amy Pond, and I am usually River Song since I am studying Archaeology!).

And it doesn't stop there. Both of their rooms are Doctor Who themed from top to bottom with memories of all the activities we have done, shows we have seen and actors from the show we have met. Their over active imaginations and love for the show have landed them local fame in and around our town as many have come to know them simply as the Doctors. Then there is Tadd with all the countless drawings and spiral note books filled with Doctor Who doodles. I tell people to remember Tadd because one day he will be involved with Doctor who somehow, and I really believe that with all my heart.

I really must say thank you to the creators and writers of Doctor Who. It has allowed me to bond with family members and more importantly share in my children's experiences and memories. I have such a strong and unique bond with my oldest son Tadd, and we do everything we can together as Doctor and assistant. Recently we have done a sponsored virtual Doctor Who walk to raise money for the Boston marathon victims. Tadd walked one mile and I walked 13.1 miles. We also attended our first BBC Proms (Doctor Who of course!) and have donated money for getting an actual TARDIS into space later this year. We have shared many cosplay days and met our heroes together. A mother couldn't ask for more. The memories that we share will last forever, captured in countless pictures, and I wouldn't have it any other way.

And to think that it all started with a Dalek. Who would have thought?

An Amazing Journey

By Lionel Mendonsa, aged 16, from Dubai

My story with Doctor Who starts, depending on how you look at it, either in 2008 or in 2013 (because you know, wibbly-wobbly, timey-wimey!). A friend wrote an article for a magazine comparing Doctor Who to Star Trek. There was one catch, though - nobody had seen Doctor Who at the time. So, the aforementioned friend started watching it, and recommended that I watch it, and I decided to follow her advice...

Best decision ever.

I started watching Series 5 and after two and a half episodes, I was hooked. Today I am utterly obsessed with the show and luckily for me, quite a few of my friends are Whovians. They're my *Who-mies*!

In the two months that I've been watching Doctor Who, it's become more than just a show. Like Star Wars, Top Gear and Harry Potter, it's earned a special place in my heart. I've laughed at the Doctor, laughed with the Doctor, tried not to blink whenever the Weeping Angels come on screen, cried (more like mentally screamed) when Amy and Rory had to leave, cried (almost literally) when David Tennant whispered *"I don't want to go"*, and freaked out at the 'empty' child...

Because whenever I watch an episode of Doctor Who, it's like I'm *living* it, like I'm actually *experiencing* everything that's happening in it.

It's been an amazing journey with the Doctor and it's not going to stop any time soon.

The Moral Compass

By Christie Dominic Inman-Hall, aged 21, from the UK

"What're you up to?" I asked.

"I'm just about to watch Doctor Who, if you're interested?" replied Dad.

"What's that then?"

"It's a programme about a man who travels through time in a big, blue phone box," he stated, matter of factly.

"Well, okay then. I've got nothing to lose."

"I was fourteen years old when that conversation took place. The year was 2006 and the episode in question was *New Earth*, David Tennant's first (proper) outing as the Doctor.

As I sat there, watching intrigued and enraptured, I suddenly found something stirring deep inside me. Something about this quirky, madcap programme struck a chord and from that moment on I was well and truly hooked.

I became an avid fan and watched and re-watched any episodes I could get my hands on, be they from 2005 or 1963. It honestly made no difference, just so long as, somewhere in there, there was a madman with a blue box saving the universe. Age fourteen was a difficult year for me and, if I'm honest, Doctor Who affected me deeply. I'd go so far as to say it impacted on my development into the man I am today. When I lacked guidance and drive, the Doctor was there to offer it. He became a moral compass, a counsellor and a friend. An ideal to strive for. While I may never be a time-travelling alien, I could certainly aim to be as helpful and good-natured as the Doctor.

While, of course that's an almost impossible ideal, it gave me something to work towards, and, at such a turbulent time in one's life, that's often the best thing to have. It allowed me an escape - no longer did I have to think about my chronic acne or my fumbling uselessness with the opposite sex. Now I could imagine worlds and planets and people beyond that of our small blue marble suspended in space. Now I could picture myself up there, wearing a long coat, shouting *"Allons-y!"* and saving the universe with a beautiful companion by my side.

I know that sounds desperate but when I was younger, I really did struggle with people and, by watching the Doctor in all his eccentricities, I learned that you didn't have to be nervous and awkward in your intelligence. No, in fact, you could revel in it. You could become the very life and soul of the party.

While, occasionally, I'd lose my way in such troubled-teenage-times, the Doctor never judged nor did he mind. He understood, most crucially of all, that we're only human after all. He was always there, every Saturday night, right when I needed him.

My obsession with Doctor Who is so great that, as opposed to remembering times in my life through music or photographs, my most vivid memories come when I see past episodes on television. I'm instantly transported to that time in my life and I can't help but remember all my trials and tribulations, all the silly little things that seemed so important at the time, but now seem like nothing at all. Doctor Who has been a constant facet of my life ever since that fateful day in 2006 and I honestly wouldn't change that for the world. No other programme can take you through all of time and space, give you a moral lesson, make you laugh, cry and fear for your life all at the same time. That's the wonder of Doctor Who.

Now as I sit here, older and wiser than I was in 2006, I realise that I don't need the Doctor to be my moral compass quite as often as I did. However, what I have noticed, though, is that if ever I need a pick-me-up, an adventure, a scare, a laugh, a cry, a lecture or just some ruddy fun silliness, I can always turn to Doctor Who to deliver all that and more.

Yes, the Doctor has changed his face, but everybody changes as they grow old. I know for a fact I'm indistinguishable from the fourteen year old I was when the Doctor and I first met. Friends understand that, whether they are nine-hundred year old Time Lords or not.

A Norwegian Whovian's Fairytale

By Mia Birgitte Grendal, aged 22, from Norway

Once upon a time in a land far, far north known as Norway, a 14 year old girl was sitting in her living room. It was September of 2005 and on TV was a British show that she had never heard of before. The girl watched it and kept on watching even though her younger sister was terrified of the monsters. Little did the girl know how much this show would impact her life later on...

The Norwegian Broadcasting Corporation decided to not air any more Doctor Who and the girl quickly forgot about the show about a man in a blue box. Until 2007, when she rediscovered him and fell in love. The girl had always loved all things British and in 2009 she moved to England for a year to attend a British school. Unfortunately her host family didn't own a television and the girl couldn't watch Doctor Who in the show's own country.

A couple of years later, in 2011, the girl started university and had to move away from her family. The two years that followed would turn out to be the hardest years the girl had ever experienced. Depression, anxiety and a panic disorder slowly took over her life. But in the midst of all the darkness was a little ball of light and its name was Doctor Who. Whenever everyday life became too hard, the girl would watch her Doctor travel through time and space. She would dream of him at night and wake up with a smile. Her mother would suggest that she spent some time watching the Time Lord when she could tell her daughter was falling apart.

Eventually the girl got better and she continues to get better every single day. Since she started running with the Doctor, the girl has had the pleasure of experiencing several Doctor Who related events, including *The Crash of the Elysium*, the *Doctor Who Experience*, and the *Doctor Who Proms* at the Royal Albert Hall. Experiences like these help the girl through darker periods of her life. She thinks of the Doctor as her hero, her knight in shining armour who saved her from the monsters, the good wizard in her fairy tale, and she loves him very much.

This girl's name was Mia Birgitte, and I am her. And I am proud that say that after all these years, I still am and will forever be a Whovian.

The Makings of a Teenage Whovian

By Matthew Ross, aged 16, from England

Doctor Who was introduced to me in 2006, when a friend told me he fancied Rose Tyler. He came from a Whovian family, whereas I did not. That night was the night Rose Tyler left Doctor Who. So, weirdly the first ever episode I watched was Rose's last, *Doomsday*. Having seen the two biggest villains in the show fight each other I wanted more. I waited patiently for *The Runaway Bride* whilst my friend filled me in on the show's history

When Christmas came around I sat and loved every second. Catherine Tate was exactly the companion needed to keep my interests going, I remember screaming at the TV for her to accept the Doctor's offer, but I and so many others settled for Martha Jones. As Series 3 ended and John Simm appeared playing the Master, my interest in the Classic Series perked up.

After doing a bit of research I was recommended the episode that started my teacher's Whovian interests and that Christmas I knew what I wanted - *The Five Doctors*. The first ever Classic Series story I watched was an epic. Seeing the first five-ish Doctors working together against Borusa was amazing. The whole idea of a rebel leaving to explore and help the universe hooked me in. I became a Whovian. Each and every birthday and Christmas after that I got a little piece of history. More and more Doctors were introduced to me, until I found my favourite. Tom Baker.

The teeth, scarf, curls and jelly babies did it for me. Seeing him fight Davros in *Genesis of the Daleks*, battle Sutek in *Pyramids of Mars* and offer jelly babies to bemused Daleks was brilliant. He had a presence no other Doctor has matched. Funny and serious, he is and forever will be my Doctor. So imagine the look of glee on my face when, on my 16th birthday a few days ago, I unwrapped a scarf. My grandma had got me the official replica of Tom Baker's scarf.

Thank you, WhovianNet, for doing this book, I have loved reminiscing. 'Whovian' is without a doubt the best title to have.

We shall go on, for Doctor Who can never end, as long as humans have imagination...

Why Hello There, Doctor!

By Jessica Goldberg, aged 15, from the USA

Maybe it was a coincidence that I happened to be born 23rd November. Maybe it's just a coincidence that's the same day that Doctor Who first aired, all those years ago. I do believe it's a good kind of coincidence though. One that began to shape my life nearly 15 years ago.

My sonic began shaking, shaking so violently that it tore itself from my grasp. That's when I met him, all chin and lanky frame. His words of space adventure and random questions about bananas. He swept me away claiming that we were the last Time Lords in existence, and saying we would travel the universe for the rest of our lives.

That's how I met him, and truth be told I entered his ship, learned all of his aliens. I even watched as the two of us were joined by countless companions. They were fun and kept him from making stupid decisions. The sad thing was that they all had to say goodbye, but I've never had to. He won't let me leave like the others, and I don't want to.

The Doctor and I, the battling duo. I know all his catch phrases, his favorite clothes. Whenever I came home he always came with me, I soon showed him to my family. Then he introduced me to my friends, we all had caught the Doctor Bug. We'd recited his adventures and dueled with his enemies.

The Doctor found me friends, the Doctor found me love. The love of friendship, the love known as trust. Without his help, without his countless adventures, I wouldn't have my fellow Whovians. These people who I've depended my life on, and never knew I needed as much as I do.

I laughed at his jokes, as I usually did. His soft amber eyes always looked at me when I laughed. They always seemed happier when they gazed at me. Others might tell you it's because we are the last remaining Time Lords. I don't agree. It's because I love the Doctor and he loves me.

As you can see I deeply love the Doctor, his advice has helped me through the hardest of times. Maybe that coincidence was just what I needed. That pick me up, the kind that comes in a little blue box. That mad man, mad as he might be, found me friends, gave me hope, and showed me love. That kind of Time Lord love that will live within me forever, and won't need to regenerate. And that wonderful coincidence is why I say *"Allons-y"*!

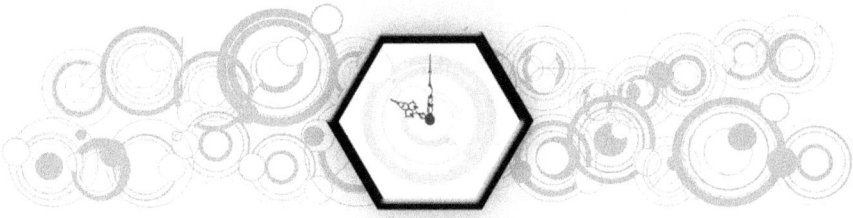

Werewolves and Time Lords

By Declan Fairey, aged 16, from the UK

For as long as I can remember, I have always been drawn towards the strange, the mysterious and the magical. It is therefore no surprise that when I first discovered Doctor Who, I quickly became a big fan. But the story of how I first came to watch an episode of the show is one with many twists and turns...

My very first encounter with the Doctor that I can even vaguely remember was the short Children in Need episode broadcast in November 2005. Back then, at the age of nine, the whole thing just left me thoroughly confused. I witnessed one man suddenly change into another, and then proceed to act like a maniac in what appeared to be a rather funny looking house. I can hardly be blamed for being left somewhat befuddled!

My Mum and Dad, however, clearly recognised the show, though they had not watched it since their own childhoods. My Mum turned to me and said, "Doctor Who, Declan! You'd like that - it's just up your street!"

For my part, I wasn't so sure. This seemed a little odd, even for my tastes. But nevertheless a part of me remained intrigued. And it wasn't long before I truly entered the world of Doctor Who for the first time.

In April 2006, whilst casually watching TV, I saw a trailer for the Doctor Who episode *Tooth and Claw*. And one aspect of it jumped out from it - the *werewolf!*

My interest in werewolves had been piqued by reading and later watching the film of *Harry Potter and the Prisoner of Azkaban*. They had introduced me to the concept of a werewolf, and I was thoroughly fascinated. I therefore made a point of watching this show (whose name I had not yet bothered to memorise) for the single purpose of seeing another take on the myth.

And so it was that on the 22nd April 2006, me and my family sat down to watch our first episode of Doctor Who together. By the time the credits rolled and that incredible music sounded once more, the werewolf was the last thing on my mind. Instead my mind had been set racing by this mysterious "Doctor" and his companion. And if I was certain of one thing, it was that I would be watching again next week...

Over the ensuing couple of months I met Sarah Jane Smith and K-9, peered through a fireplace from the future to the past, came face to face with the Cybermen and was scared witless by the Devil himself. Then came the Daleks, and there was no going back.

Doctor Who had become a part of my life.

In time, companions came and went. Eventually so did my first incarnation of the Doctor. But at its heart, so many of the aspects of the show that enchanted me so thoroughly then still stay true to this day.

Adventure. Exploration. Friendship. Danger. Monsters. Mystery. Doctor *who*?

And I wouldn't have it any other way.

I Heart The Doctor

By Destiny Nicole Blackston, aged 7, from the USA

My name is Destiny. I am 7 years old. I come from USA. My favourite Doctor is the Tenth. I've seen all of the Eighth and Ninth and the end of the Seventh. My favourite companions who travelled with the Doctor are Rose and Martha. Rose is pretty and sweet and she's always excited to go on adventures. Martha is beautiful and kind and she was training to be a doctor and I want to be a doctor when I grow up.

At first when I was watching Doctor Who I thought I wouldn't like it and I thought it was crazy but as soon as I watched it I liked it. It was unique and weird but pretty interesting. Just to let you know I cried when the Doctor changed into a different Doctor and when Rose left. The Doctor really misses Rose and my Mama, my sister and my step dad were choking up too.

My favourite episode is *Dalek* because I got to see what was inside a Dalek and it was cute and Rose didn't get killed.

Doctor Who?

By Bérénice Pirlot, aged 17, from Belgium

When I first met the Doctor, I was just a 13 years old Belgian who did not see immediately in him the help she needed to get through school and her problems.

I was looking at my grandmother's telly thinking, "Why is this very strange man getting out of a police box with a ginger woman? Why is he running to the girl who appeared on the street? What's this screaming robot? Is "The Doctor" even a name?!" I did not understand anything, but I wanted to know what was going to happen next. I thought I would never know. Then... I forgot.

About a year later, I saw strips about Ten, Jack and the Daleks on deviantArt. I was curious. I remembered watching the show once. So I looked up on a French website for the latest news and found a clip of *The End of Time* which had been aired two months earlier. Blimey, it was not as strange as in my memories! That's how I started Doctor Who. It all began and everything changed.

The Doctor immediately took me to the stars. I met a mad man with a box, sad and broken because of the Time War and everyone he lost, but always amazed by new life forms and everything he saw, new or not. A man who, despite all the bad things that happens to him, keeps going on and never loses hope. Exactly the kind of character I would love and needed to escape my world, so grey and unhappy outside home.

The Doctor made me discover planets, aliens and companions who made me dream and forget. The show became my world, my secret garden. I could not stop talking and thinking about it, trying to give people the curiosity to watch it too. I wanted to meet someone who loved it as much as me. But I live in Belgium and here, on the French-speaking side of the country, there are really not a lot of Whovians. It took me three years and a half to find about 50 fans on Facebook, when on the Flemish group they are 500. I met one Whovian. As for the ones I know outside the Internet, it is me who made them watch it. I felt alone, but special for loving something awesome that not many people knew about.

The Doctor gives hope. He gives trust. He gives dreams. He reminds us that even if he's not perfect and makes mistakes, he goes on trying to be a good person. He becomes an imaginary friend for who we care as if he was real.

We know he's not. But we can keep believing and dreaming of him, letting him help us getting through our problems if what we learn from him can make things easier.

I was 13 when I met him. I was 14 when I started following him and his companions into their adventures. Now I'm 17, soon 18. I went from the end of my childhood to my teenage years and now to the beginning of my legally adult life with him. I grew up with the Doctor by my side.

Recently I went to see a psychologist because of school problems. That's when I realised the Doctor did more than helping me. I knew that I could have end up depressive without the show and everything it brings to me.I'm still very, very shy, but I don't care about not being dressed like everyone else. I wear Doctor Who t-shirts, jeans and converses, I don't like shopping, make-up, modern music, getting drunk, smoking and stuff like that. I'm proud of not being like most of the young people of my age. Because the Doctor taught me that everyone is important, that I am the way I am and that being different is not a bad thing. Like him, I'm sad when I'm feeling alone. But I never really am. I know he's kind of here, holding my hand, not letting go, and ready to whisper into my ear.

"Run!"

To The Mad Man, With Love

By Camille, aged 20, France

The first nineteen years of my life, I was just a normal girl. And then, I met him. The Doctor. Doctor Who? One could ask. Well, let me tell you that this is a long (though fantastic) story. Being a Whovian is an incredible adventure. Let me show you why.

One of my closest friends had discovered the series and could not stop talking about it, sending me videos and funny quotes, saying it was her favourite show. However, it was a long time before I entered the TARDIS for the first time. But thanks to chance and Shakespeare, I finally joined the fandom in 2013 and I have no regrets, although I wish I had known the series sooner. The sooner the better, don't you think? Before, I had the impression that this series was a bit... mad. And in fact, I still think that this series is mad but in a good and cool way. In fact, this madness is actually good for my health (whereas my family cannot get that a Dalek is frightening and that bow ties are cool). I do have the impression that now I belong to another world, to the Whovian world, a fantastic world.

For me, the Doctor is not simply a mad time traveller in a blue box. He means a lot to me and I pray every night for his TARDIS to land on my lawn and for him to invite me on his trips through time and space. In many ways, he is a hero, a unique one, a crazy one, a lovely one.

When I watch Doctor Who, I have this amazing feeling that I enter a new world, leaving the routine behind me (which is good sometimes). This series is always surprising and all the more addictive. One can never guess what's going on or what joke the Doctor is going to make or on what sort of planet he has just arrived. The series always reinvents itself. When I have a (rare) feeling of déjà vu, I actually realise that I was wrong because some detail makes the episode totally different. It's so thrilling to always rediscover the show or to see another particularity (should I say 'craziness'?) of the Doctor... I mean, only a few series or films are able to do such amazing wonders...

I really love this raggedy man. He may be a Time Lord, he has become really humane and human throughout the series. He's just incredible, improbable and extraordinary. I like the fact that he refuses to have weapons and despises people having guns. Furthermore, a screwdriver is really nicer than

The Doctor has totally transformed my life forever. I now want to explore the universe more than ever, which has always been one of my secret fantasies and should probably have remained a secret dream because now another thing is clear: I'm a bit like the the Doctor. Mad. Indeed, how can I explore the universe if I haven't got a TARDIS? Not to mention time travelling... It's going to be really complicated but I'll get by.

Furthermore, I am French and, you know, the Doctor and his TARDIS are not really popular in France. People liking them are quite rare or presented as being strange but I really don't care and I am proud to be different from my countrymen if that only means I have noticed what's really good with being part of the Doctor Who family. May the journey never end.

From Hate to Love

By Jade Kelly, aged 15, from England

I hated it. I really did. My brother would steal the remote every Saturday and turn on the TV to watch Doctor Who. I would sigh and flick through a princess-y magazine whilst not really paying attention to watch was playing on the TV. Then one day I did. *The Shakespeare Code*. That was it. I was hooked. Every week I would join my little brother and be enticed by the adventures of the Doctor and his companion. Eventually I went back and watched all the episodes from the Ninth Doctor and fell in love with Rose.

Although my first regeneration didn't quite go smoothly. Let's face it, the Tenth Doctor was my first Doctor and he will always have a place in my heart, so when the line *"I don't want to go"* was said, my heart was torn into a million little pieces. When Eleven came along, I didn't want to hear any of it, I simply refused to watch Series 5. That is until BBC Three decided to replay it. Eleven was simply amazing and I regretted not watching him when he first came on.

Shipping. It wasn't a thing that I was particularly familiar with until I watched Ten and Rose together. Now I ship everyone together, 11 and River, Amy and Rory, Jack and... well, everyone

Until I joined Twitter I never considered myself part of the fandom. Then on one rainy afternoon my whole life changed. I found people that understood Doctor Who like I did, people that would find the Doctor just as awesome as I did. And that's when I joined the fandom. Twitter was just the beginning - today, fan videos, fan fic, and Trock are all part of my daily life.

So, how has Doctor Who affected my life? How *hasn't* it would be a better question to answer. I can't walk down the street without making a Doctor Who reference. I can't stay in the dark, I simply have to stare at stone statues, and spacesuits will never be the same. I have to check my arms for tally marks and look out for Bad Wolf signs. I check for broken clocks that tick and I listen for the TARDIS noise all the time (sometimes I think I hear it but when I look, it's gone - damn time travel!).

Doctor Who has changed my life for the better, being a Whovian means the world to me... even if I get a paranoid in the dark!

Regenerating with the Doctor

By Jane Ganberg, aged 15, from Russia

This story starts five years ago with a girl who loved creating stories for herself. She used to sit in the garden, look at the sky and imagine all sort of things. But one day, on 22nd June 2008, her stories didn't seem to go the right way. She got bored and decided to join her best friend who was watching Doctor Who. Everything changed in that girl's life.

The first episode she saw was *The Impossible Planet*. She didn't even watch it from the start but she got hooked. I am not really sure what caught her eye but what she understood was this story was one she had to follow. I cannot be certain about the moment when she fell in love with Doctor Who, but when *Doomsday* came she was already crazy about the show and the characters and she cried more than her friend ever saw her cry.

But her friend left the next week and she was too scared to watch Doctor Who on her own (half of the previous episodes had been spent under the blanket). She had fallen in love with the music already that what she did was simple - she watched the first two or three minutes until the titles and listened to the Doctor Who theme.

Slowly and gradually the Internet has entered the girl's life and Doctor Who was one of the first things she entered into the search bar. She watched different episodes in proper timey-wimey-wibbly-wobbly order but that way worked perfectly for her. By the time of the Tenth Doctor's regeneration, she had caught up with all the episodes (excluding the Classics) and had made a decision that would change her life. She was going to watch the new episodes without subtitles because for those you had to wait and she couldn't afford waiting.

Doctor Who is constantly changing and so am I. But one thing stays the same, it has always had and will always have a big part my heart, definitely bigger than any TV show or book or film has ever had. And I will always be very proud to be a Whovian.

Doctor Who helped that girl learn English, introduced her to a lot of new and awesome things and made her believe that miracles *can* happen. It helped her meet lots of great people and taught her the best lessons in life, it helped her become wiser and braver and better.

That girl became me.

The Mad Man With A Box

By Steve Rollins, aged 19, from West Virginia, USA

The Last of the Time Lords,
A Good Man Goes to War,
Upon The Eleventh Hour,
And victory's in store.
Then The Beast Below awakens,
Lets out a sounding roar,
And then The Forest of the Dead
Isn't silent anymore.
The Doctor rushes to his TARDIS,
And throws it into gear.
Then with a *WHOOSH* it vanishes,
And goes back in time a year.

It landed on The Stolen Earth,
Where The Doctor found a Rose,
A Noble, and another doc
Who went by Martha Jones.
They fought to save the human race
From the Daleks in Manhattan
Then left the world to see the stars
And find out what was happenin'
In places like The Satan Pit,
The Planet of the Ood,
And others like Utopia
Where people shan't be rude.

Then he took them back to Earth,
Because it was a Journey's End,
And The End of Time was coming,
A fact he hoped to mend.
He said, "I really hate to leave you,
But we'll never meet again.
My Rose, my Doc, and my Noble girl,
You've all become my friend."
To The Sound of Drums, he whisked away
To where? Only he knew.
And there they saw that fateful day,
The last of Doctor Who.

Introducing the Doctor

By Robyn Hilt, aged 24, from South Korea

As an American, I discovered Doctor Who one night while surfing through *Netflix* on my Wii in 2011. Now it's hard to imagine a world without Daleks and Weeping Angels. I live in fear of wi-fi and my own fat. This is why, despite being granted a Fulbright Teaching Grant to teach at an all boys school in South Korea, I eagerly awaited each air date of each episode of Series 7.

Doctor Who became my escape from culture shock. I figured that if the Doctor's companions could adjust to completely different planets, time streams, and face terrifying monsters, I could handle living in a country where I spoke only a small amount of the language. Although sometimes it felt like I was battling a pod of Cybermen who just wanted to upgrade me for a Korean speaking model, I, like all the companions before me, found my place and adapted to my new life.

During my student's English listening midterms, they were required to listen to and answer questions based upon a dialogue read by British accented woman. They said that this was the most difficult part of the test and that almost everyone missed the questions in this section. It was obvious that my students needed to be exposed to some more British accents and what better way is there to practice listening to British English than to watch Doctor Who?

I decided to watch *The Eleventh Hour* with my students and I found the episode with Korean subtitles. Not only did they get to practice listening to British accents, but also the Scottish, Amelia Pond. From the first moment my boys were riveted. They were fascinated by the idea of regeneration. They laughed at Matt Smith's disgust for Western food and were amused and slightly disgusted by fish custard. They thought that the word "Geronimo" was awesome and felt Amy's anger at being forced to wait 14 years to go travelling with the Doctor. They groaned when class ended and demanded more.

Weeks later my boys tell me that they've been watching more episodes and complain that they aren't getting their homework done because they are too busy watching Doctor Who. Some have even picked their own favourite Doctor.

This is proof that Doctor Who is a TV show that has the power to not only unite generations, but cultures as well.

Dear Doctor

By Aishwarya Iyer, aged 16, from Dubai

Dear Doctor,

Hello there, I'm a little girl living in the Middle East. You probably don't know me, but that's the point of it all, isn't it? Now that your journey has come to its grand 50, I thought I would write to you telling you how much your antics really mean to me.

It's funny, but I really didn't intend to get to know you at first. It was a year ago, when I was asked to write an entertainment article for my school's science magazine. I enjoy writing but science and me don't go to well, so I knew that this was a huge responsibility. After hours of searching on the Internet (this huge world-in-a-world kind of thing, I don't get it but I guess it gives you the answer to everything. Except the important life questions...), I found a topic I could actually wager on. The raging battle between the two biggest television series enterprises of all times - Star Trek and Doctor Who. But there was just this one problem, I had never watched either.

You see I didn't really see the big problem in bluffing right then. So I researched all over the net and found the basic statistics needed to support the article. Surprisingly nobody ever figured out that I had absolutely no idea what I was talking about in the article, but the article was a big hit nonetheless. You know how life plays a really weird trick on you. Suddenly when you are trying so hard to forget something, it pops up everywhere. That's what happened. Your pictures, dialogues, interviews, scene clippings, even episode links landed up everywhere. It was quite annoying for a while. But like every other companion, I was swept away by all that curiosity and that's how I landed on the very first episode that the Eleventh Doctor did.

Pretty soon, I was just like the little red-headed girl. I didn't know the Doctor but there was something that compelled me to keep watching, something that forced me to patiently wait and figure out who this really was. Maybe that's how it all started, when I couldn't figure you out. I always understand people, that's my specialty, but not with you. You threw me off balance, I never knew what the Doctor would do next, and that is what made me stay.

With every journey, there came a mystery, there came a dilemma, there came a situation where all my moral opinions went for a toss. Most of the times I sided with the Doctor, but there were other times were I shouted at the fool (granted, that you couldn't hear me) asking him, "What the hell do you think you're doing?". But you always got me dumbfounded at the end. That's what I hated about you the most. I did not like being proven wrong.

So, Doctor, the Eleventh specifically, this is not goodbye. No, it never could be. This is a letter, the dusty old yellow paper kind, which you store away in your library, so another Clara could find it. It's that wisp of memory that you always tell yourself you don't need to look back to, but you end up stumbling on it anyway, and then you can't stop. It's that piece of I-Love-You, when you don't know if it's the tears or the smiles that matter.

Let me tell you, as I write this letter, I have a bit of both right now. And you know what, Doctor? I wouldn't have it any other way. So sleep well my child, the world will sing you the lullaby and when you wake up once again, we will still be here helping you up on your feet.

Yours Truly,
The Unknown Companion

P.S. You did make it a good story in the end.

Doctor What?

By Clarissa, aged 15, from Hong Kong

"Doctor what?" had always been my reaction when my friends talked about the show, because even as we date back to as soon as half a year ago, I have never watched a single episode.

I have friends who were hardcore fans of Doctor Who from pretty much a few years back (and by hardcore you know I mean those who are knee-deep in merchandise) but despite that, I never really gave much thought on watching it. I had TV shows I was already obsessed with so I let my friends scream at me about exciting news related to their show, they let me do the same, and we were happy the way things were.

And that had been the way it was for the longest time, until one night, I got a bit bored. Actually, 'a bit' would have been an understatement. I had absolutely nothing to do then, so I thought I would check the show out for a bit, maybe get to know the characters and then I assumed I would just move on with my life.

But... *Spoiler alert!* I didn't.

I started watching the show mid-series by starting on *The Eleventh Hour*, since during that time, they were airing episodes with Eleven in them and my friends thought that would have been a good place to start. So I got comfy and started the journey without giving much thought to it and just thinking I could pass some time. But I got hooked onto it quickly and soon I was streaming the episodes one by one without stopping. And by the time I was done, I realised I had gone through a ton of episodes and it was nearly three in the morning.

I never thought sci-fi would appeal to me and I thought the show really was about one thing - Science and science only, but then it turned out I was wrong and I fell in love with the characters soon enough.

To any sane person out there, I probably have wasted a ton of time and energy devoting myself to the fictional characters and wanting to hang out in places that aren't even existent, but to me, even if that world out there is made up, it's good enough. I'm constantly awaiting a blue box to show up outside my house and for the mad man inside it to whisk me away may seem absurd.

A girl can dream, right?

How I Met the Doctor

By Gerlinde, aged 17, from the Netherlands

I started watching Doctor Who because I had heard quite a lot about it on *YouTube*. People even made songs about it, so I figured that it must be worth it. So in September 2012, when I basically just wanted something to escape school, I started watching it. In about a month I watched the whole new Doctor Who series. I basically fell in love. I couldn't wait to get home from school and watch more and I was totally besotted. Then Christmas came and I saw my first ever live Doctor Who episode and it honestly made my Christmas.

Apart from just watching the series, I also got on the Internet and saw so many people who also are a fan of Doctor Who and they made the experience even better. They showed me the things that I had missed while watching the episodes and they explained me things and I learned more and more. Then I also started watching the Classic Doctor Who. I'm nowhere near finishing that, because it's a lot to watch, but it has made me fall even more in love with the Doctor, the show and just the messages that it gives.

I don't really have a favourite Doctor yet. All of them are the Doctor for me, they might be different at some points, but there also the same man and I just keep falling in love.

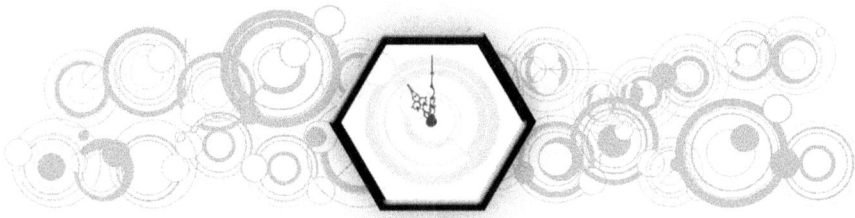

Friends and Strangers

By Vanessa Cordova, aged 21, from Arizona, Phoenix

Doctor Who has definitely changed my life. I feel like now I have something to talk about with people. I look back at my life before Doctor Who and my life now and it feels weird to think of not knowing The Doctor, Amy Pond, and the TARDIS. But I know I can't wait to see all the new adventures with The Doctor, all the places he goes and the companions he meets.

What I love about Doctor Who is that I get to talk about it with everyone and I have even introduced Doctor Who to my family. The first time I heard about the show was when I was looking online, so I am grateful to now be apart of this amazing fandom. I now find myself talking about the show with my family, friends, and strangers. Because we all have something in common, and it's are love for the show. The characters are so amazing they make us care what happens to them. The actors and writers make it enjoyable and believable. And for us as fans, we feel that it can really happen, that the TARDIS will land in our back yard and we'll get to eat fish fingers and custard with the Doctor...

The Fandom and I

By Elaine M. aged 21, from the Philippines

I started watching in March 2013 when my brother copied a bunch of anime shows and along with them, the complete roundup of Series 5 episodes. But I've actually been curious about the show since a friend of mine who lives in Wales mentioned it years ago and more recently, online friends of mine who are fans.

So on I went to watch the mentioned series and I was fascinated by the universe which the Doctor revolves in. So I set out to download and watch all the modern series and by the time this is published, I'll have finished Series 7.

I have to say I'm just as fascinated by the fandom. It is such a dedicated, creative, awesome bunch. And as I've seen during the Twelfth Doctor announcement, the fandom can GIF, photoset, quote, and just post things pretty darn fast (since I got hooked on the show I've been a solid Tumblr lurker). I now have another reason to visit the UK - some location sightseeing and going to look for real blue police boxes to take photos with. It's awesome too how this passion which we have in common has already reached 50 years.

In the episodes I've seen I've learned lessons which hopefully I can apply to real life. I've cried and cheered countless times over the Doctor, his friends and companions. I also show some love for the villains. I came along in time for the 50th anniversary year and it's such an exciting time - the first time I'm watching a series with everyone else and I get to see a new Doctor. It'll be bittersweet seeing Matt Smith go this Christmas though, but as some say, we must be open to new possibilities. I'm so looking forward to seeing Peter Capaldi work that TARDIS and go on many adventures. I don't know much about him but I think he'll do splendidly.

I'm not even sure if any channel in my country, whether on cable or Freeview, shows Doctor Who, so bless the Internet folks. Since Philippine fans are still pretty rare in general, it's great to have met a good few local fellows in Doctor Who through WhovianNet. I hope to remain a fan until the end of time.

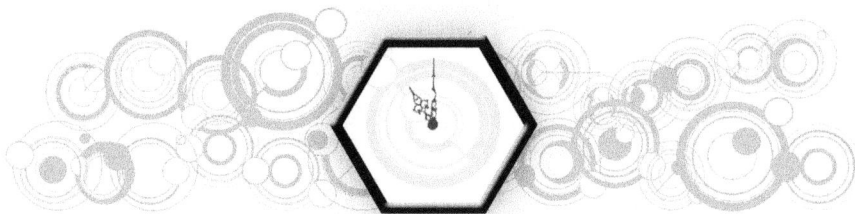

The Adventure of Life

By Frankky Hightower, aged 12, from the USA

First, let me say a few things. I haven't been watching Doctor Who that long. Approximately 9 to 10 months. But in the first month I had watched the whole of the episodes from 2006 on up. Even seeing some episodes two or three times along with some of the Classic series and the TV Movie. So, I would consider myself a die hard Whovian. Alright, now that that's clear, I would love to discuss the impact Doctor Who has made upon me.

Let's pretend for a moment you're an actor with a deep interest in physics. So of course things like *Star Trek* and *The Hitchhiker's Guide to the Galaxy* keep you watching and reading them for hours on end. And you read and you read and you watch and you watch. And you're obsessed with these stories and they're great and all, but something is missing. You talk about them and about your favourite thing that happened in the story, but you can't be *part* of it. It's there on the other side of a pane of glass, but you can't *feel* it and *experience* it.

That's what makes me love Doctor Who. You can be *inside* the TARDIS, traveling through all of time and space. You can be Amy. You can be Jack. You can be Donna. You can be Sarah Jane. You can even be the lone Time Lord with a blue box. You feel their pain and their excitement. You are on that stage pretending to be those characters and, eventually, *becoming* them.

You slave through each week just to see one little episode and you wait for that unbelievable man to fly down and welcome you aboard. But he never does. So you wait longer, and you pray and you wish and you finally have to come to face facts. He's not coming. And then you remember how you're an actor and how you dream at night. And then you make a decision, a decision that will change your life, that you have to create your own adventure...

This is me. And this is why I have decided to make life as interesting as possible and to be my own hero. This is by far the most important thing Doctor Who has taught me so far. I'm making my life an adventure and hey, maybe one day I'll get to be on Doctor Who, running through corridors with danger around every corner.

What do I know? The universe is full of miracles.

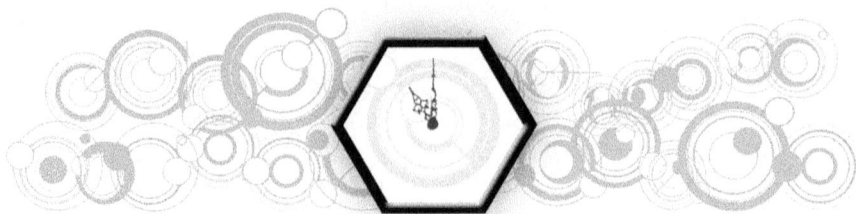

My Time Travel Adventure

By Anne Pagkalinawan, aged 16, from the Philippines

I met the Doctor whilst on a road trip with my cousins. One of our destinations had been a cemetery which was surrounded by stone angels. I sensed fear coming from my two older cousins and suddenly they whispered to us, *"Don't blink"*. They told us about the Weeping Angels in *Blink* and *The Angels Take Manhattan*. At first, I thought they were mad. How could stone angels do such a thing? One of them told me then about Doctor Who and how it changed her perspective of time travel and all things around her. I got curious really. Who wouldn't? A handsome Time Lord with a pretty companion. I knew I'd like it, but I never thought I'd love it...

Going back to my home town, I went to all my local DVD stores and asked for Doctor Who until I went to a local market and found people selling Seasons 1 to 4. I immediately bought them without hesitation and started watching it.

A few months later, I was hooked. My friends have even noticed how in love I am with my Doctor. Needless to say, I use Doctor Who references all the time!

Who Tube

By Amanda McKenna, aged 17, from the USA

Growing up, most kids I knew were afraid of monsters and scary stories, but I *lived* off them. Living in America, the sci-fi time travelling adventure that is Doctor Who never graced my TV screen. Upon entering my 'tween' years, though, I discovered a website called *YouTube*. As well as introducing me to a new way of thinking and an outlet to express my creativity, it also introduced my ears to a genre of music called Time Lord Rock - music created by fans of Doctor Who about Doctor Who.

Still in my early years of being a teen and not yet acquiring the teenage 'fangirl' tendencies, I didn't scour the Internet to watch this show that everyone was singing about. Instead I had melodies upon melodies stuck in my head of Sally Sparrow, not blinking and adventures through time. Even though I didn't know what the lyrics meant, I frequently immersed myself in them for years to come.

Fast forward to a 15 year old me on summer break and the mystical show I had become familiar with through music pops on my TV guide. Unbeknownst to me, the show was currently in its fifth season and had reached its American audience. I fell in love with it at my first episode - green, scaly creatures that live within the Earth's crust, some seeking revenge, some seeking alliance, and one man witnessing it all as he does what he can to make the future a harmonious place.

From the writing to the chemistry of the actors to the strange new lands, just like the companions, I craved to see more. I became a member of *Netflix* and in the months that followed I found myself in a trance, watching not only the Eleventh Doctor but a string of Doctors interact with other worlds and a variety of humans who were courageous and clever enough to join him.

When I was 16 I joined another site, *Tumblr*, due to Doctor Who. There I was able to interact with others who shared the same feelings I had for the show, people who not only loved the actors, but also the writers and those in charge of production. People who laugh while they watch Doctor Who and appreciate the witty banter in the scripts. People who see a deeper meaning and know it's not just a TV show. People who understand the idea that every life is important.

I believe that Doctor Who has lasted so long because everyone can relate. We are all created because of the string of lives that came before us on our family tree. A big reality that's not discussed in everyday life is death. One day we'll all be gone and everything will continue to progress and, unlike most sci-fi shows, Doctor Who doesn't fully glamorise the life of travelling through the stars. It shows us that people die, and not always for a cause. But their existence benefited our world in some way, whether it was just from giving one person hope or by leading the human race into the stars.

As a viewer of the show you witness just how many lives are changed from coming into contact with the Doctor. Iin the past three years of being a Whovian, my life has changed, too. I've made so many new friends because we all watch the show, a lot of whom are writers and we've shared our ideas and helped each other's creativity. I've also posted some of my own ideas in video form on YouTube to a growing audience of over 10,000 subscribers. I've also developed a slight fear of statues which I'm now unable to successfully describe to my non-Whovian friends...

All in all I entered the Doctor Who world by hearing the sounds of admiration that others had for the show. With that I found friendship, a new drive to create and a positive outlook on the future. I hope to have many more adventures with the Doctor.

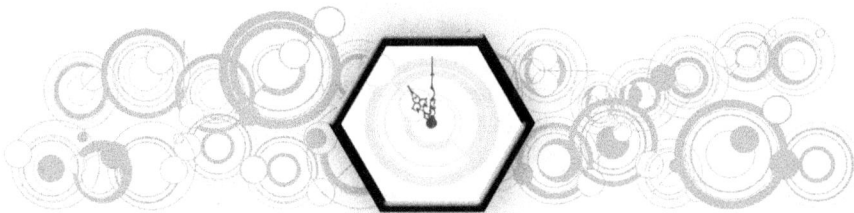

A Worthwhile Accident

By Alexandra Phillips, aged 17, from Gladewater, TX

Back in 2011, the second half of ninth grade, my algebra teacher said if we were to guess his ringtone we would get extra points on a quiz. The hints he gave us were that it orignally began airing in the 1960s and brought back in 2005 and *"that the guy who played Barty Crouch Jr. in Harry Potter played the main character at some point"*.

I'd never heard the theme to Doctor Who so for some reason I thought it the theme to *Stargate SG-1*. After revealing the answer, he told us a bit about it and because we seemed very interested in it, he showed us an episode a few days later.

Silence in the Library became the first episode of Doctor Who I ever watched. Unfortunately at that time my household did not have cable or Internet so I could never fuel the new love I had discovered. The fire was kept going by him telling us about the newest episodes.

Cut to the first week of November 2012. I find out my cousin, a fellow Whovian, will be at Thanksgiving with us. I was excited and so I decided to make her a present based on a Wassily Kandinsky quote I had found in an art magazine. It featured her favourite Doctor (Eleven) playing a keyboard. As I had no idea what he looked like, I did some research and looked up the Doctor on *Wikipedia*. Imagine my surprise when I found out how different so many of them were! Inadvertently, Matt Smith's Doctor made me fall back in love with the show and because of that I can never thank him enough.

I became a Whovian by accident but I don't regret it. It's just a wonderful experience. It's one of the oldest fandoms of the 1900s. There is just so much to watch and listen to and read and loads of the people I've interacted with have such passion for the show. I love a show with a long history. It makes it more fun. Fifty years though. Wow, just... *wow*!

Doctor Who teaches us so much about change and acceptance and love and so many other lessons and it tells us it's OK to be different. Like Christopher Eccelston said once, it shows us that when we find something scary or different it's OK to be afraid and it's OK to react with wonder. It has pulled so many people through hardships in their life and it's helped so many who have felt unimportant to realise that even in the smallest ways, you *are* important. In the nearly eighteen years that I've been alive, I've never seen another show do that for as long as Doctor Who has. And I think that's wonderful.

I've been hurt so much by others. Sometimes I get the urge to hurt those who hurt me, but I don't because I think of what the Doctor might think of me if I did. The Doctor is a legend among heroes. I believe in him, I know he's real and I know he's out there somewhere traveling the universe in his beautiful blue box, helping others and saving worlds.

Sometimes when I get upset, I'll go watch an episode or serial that I really enjoy and it'll help me feel better. I love that about the show, that it can serve as a comfort to the hurt. Thank you, Doctor Who, for being there for the ones who need it.

And thank you, WhovianNet, for allowing others to share their stories.

www.ingramcontent.com/pod-product-compliance
Lightning Source LLC
La Vergne TN
LVHW021343080426
835508LV00020B/2094